D0254221

Urban Teaching
The Essentials

REVISED EDITION

Urban Teaching
The Essentials

Lois Weiner

TEACHERS
COLLEGE
PRESS

Teachers College, Columbia University
New York and London

Published by Teachers College Press, 1234 Amsterdam Avenue, New York, NY 10027

Copyright © 2006 by Teachers College, Columbia University

All rights reserved. No part of this publication may be reproduced or transmitted in any form or by any means, electronic or mechanical, including photocopy, or any information storage and retrieval system, without permission from the publisher.

Library of Congress Cataloging-in-Publication Data

Weiner, Lois.
    Urban teaching : the essentials / Lois Weiner.–Revised ed.
      p. cm.
    ISBN-13: 978-0-8077-4643-1 (pbk. : alk. paper)
    ISBN-10: 0-8077-4643-6 (pbk. : alk. paper)
     1. Education, Urban–United States. 2. Teachers–Training of–United States. 3. Urban schools–United States. 4. Minorities–Education–United States. 5. Teaching–Social aspects–United States. I. Title.

    LC 5119.8.W45 2005
    371'.009173'2–dc22   2005050600

ISBN-13 978-0-8077-4643-1 (paper)   ISBN-10 0-8077-4643-6 (paper)

Printed on acid-free paper

Manufactured in the United States of America

13   12   11   10   09   08   07   8   7   6   5   4   3   2

❖

To my daughter, Petra

❖

Contents

Introduction

I've written this book to acquaint new and prospective city teachers with the extensive practical problems they are likely to encounter in their jobs and the weighty moral dimensions of their new occupation. The advice I offer draws on my substantial experience teaching in suburban and urban schools and on my work as a teacher educator and researcher.

My earlier book, *Preparing Teachers for Urban Schools: Lessons from Thirty Years of School Reform* (Teachers College Press, 1993)—sadly, out of print—is a scholarly work that synthesizes and analyzes research on urban teacher preparation. This volume is a more personal and subjective take on urban teaching. It is written in my voice and presents my opinions on many controversial issues. Though my ideas have been informed by my analysis of a great deal of scholarship, I have avoided citations and references for the sake of making the text as readable as possible, as close to a personal conversation as I could make it.

I have two reasons for having used this format. First, I have found that the books that have made the greatest impression on students in my education classes are those that have a clear authorial voice and present life in classrooms as teachers and students experience it. Second, I think that teachers must be critical thinkers, and in this volume I attempt to model the ways in which I hope city teachers will think about their classrooms and educational issues.

When I completed my doctorate in 1990, I worried that I would lose touch with the reality of teaching in urban schools. I think the opposite has occurred: My knowledge of urban schooling has deepened over the past years. Though I no longer have a K–12 classroom of my own, I teach college students from an astounding variety of backgrounds, many of them graduates of city schools like those in which I taught. I also work with seasoned city teachers who have returned to the university for a graduate degree that provides professional development. My students at New Jersey City University have given me far more information and insight about life in classrooms than I ever could have acquired as a classroom teacher in a single school.

This revised edition of *Urban Teaching* reflects both my recent experiences as a teacher educator and changes in schools since 1998. I decided to revise the book to deal with alterations in city schools since publication of the first edition, in particular the enormous increase in immigration, inclusion of students with special needs, the heightened emphasis on testing, and recruitment of teachers through nontraditional routes. New teachers confront a changed political climate as well, one in which the basic premises of our system of public education for more than a century are being challenged. This new edition contains material that reflects research on these changes as well as related topics. However, much of the volume remains essentially the same—as are, I would argue, the vexing problems and rich rewards of urban teaching.

❖ ❖ ❖

As was true before, my colleagues in the Department of Elementary and Secondary Education at New Jersey City University continue to inspire and teach me about urban teacher education. Neither this edition nor the first could have been written without the support of my husband, Michael Seitz, whom I can rely on for thoughtful consideration of my ideas and a good dinner when I return home from a long night of teaching. Thanks go to Brian Ellerbeck at Teachers College Press, who assisted in the production of this new edition, as he did the first.

This book is dedicated to my daughter, Petra Seitz, known to readers of the earlier edition by her childhood nickname, "Pooski." She consistently reminds me of what classroom life is like for students, and we are hopeful that this book will help improve learning in city classrooms for all kids.

Lois Weiner
New York City, January 2005

1 A Book of Advice for Prospective and New Urban Teachers

I've written this book for city teachers just starting their careers and students in education classes who want to learn about teaching successfully in urban schools. My suggestions are based on what I've learned in two careers—the first as a public school teacher, the second as a college professor and researcher on urban teacher preparation. I've found that students in my college courses can never get enough information from me about what they should be doing when they have their own classrooms; and if they don't have friends who are successful city teachers, they have no other way to obtain this "insider" advice. Nothing can substitute for actually teaching in an urban school—for experiencing the satisfactions, crises, and dilemmas—but having solid advice about what to expect and how to think about the issues can certainly help.

Sometimes the guidance new and prospective teachers receive from acquaintances who are experienced teachers is sound, but at other times the recommendations are problematic. The advice is well intentioned, and it may help a newcomer survive, but it also oversimplifies the wonderfully complex job of teaching. One example is the recommendation "Don't be friendly with the kids." New teachers who take that advice at face value sometimes avoid common mistakes, but they also miss the chance to think through precisely what kind of relationship they want to have with their students and why.

At its best, teaching in city schools is exhausting, exhilarating, frustrating, and fulfilling. In my experience, city teachers work under the most frustrating conditions and yet they have the greatest responsibility for changing and saving lives. Learning to teach under these circumstances can take several years, and during that time many new teachers leave their jobs because they feel too defeated to continue. I've written this book to help you navigate your first years as a city teacher.

I hope you consider the chapters in this book a series of conversations with a friend who taught in city schools for many years and loved her work. What would you want to learn from this experienced

3

teacher? You'd probably want a frank, thoughtful assessment about the qualities you'll need to be successful and accurate information about what to expect when you have your own classroom. In a nutshell, that's what I hope you'll learn from this book. But in order to assess the advice I'll give you, you should know more about my background. Why should you take my advice rather than the suggestions you could get from someone else? How does my advice differ from the material presented in textbooks that introduce prospective teachers to their new occupation?

The students in my college classes often say that they value my suggestions about teaching in urban schools because I am an experienced city teacher. Only a tiny percentage of college faculty who prepare teachers ever taught in urban schools. Even when the advice they give prospective teachers is accurate, teacher candidates are often suspicious that it's not rooted in a realistic assessment of what it's possible to do in a real classroom. Let me reassure you that the suggestions and ideas I present in this book reflect my 15 years of public school teaching, 7 in suburban school systems in California and New York, 8 in New York City in two very tough schools.

When I made the decision to teach in New York City, where I lived after moving from California, I knew I was in for a significant change in my teaching life; and though I was nervous, I felt confident. After all, I had been a highly regarded teacher and had enjoyed working with the "problem" kids in these schools. I was popular with students of all races and respected by colleagues. I had always enjoyed developing materials and figuring out teaching problems. I knew my subject matter, English, and had conscientiously attended to my professional development by taking many graduate courses in addition to earning a master's degree in teaching English.

What a shock I had my first semester as a city teacher! I was totally unprepared psychologically for what I faced in my first months. By November I was wracked with doubt about remaining. I felt diminished and discouraged, and for the first time since acquiring my own classroom, I questioned my teaching ability. Much of my knowledge of teaching seemed irrelevant, and I had trouble connecting with my students as people. I felt a lack of success and saw myself becoming antagonistic to my students, acting like the teachers I had vowed never to resemble.

However, by April I had begun to enjoy my students, my teaching, and my colleagues, as I had in the past. The next year I was transferred to a school with an even worse (undeservedly so) reputation. However,

I made the change with little difficulty and soon became a well liked and respected member of the faculty. Over the next decade I taught in three different schools in Manhattan and thrived as a teacher, more than I ever had in the suburbs.

I forgot about my initial introduction to urban teaching as I became accustomed to my new work environment. Occasionally I noticed that my experiences teaching in suburban schools gave me a different perspective on school practices, but I had no reason or opportunity to think about my introduction to city teaching until I began my doctoral work and examined my career. When I recalled my first months as a city teacher, several questions came to mind. Why did I find urban teaching so traumatic those first months? How did I make the adjustment? How did existing research explain my experience? How could the answers to my questions be used to help people who wanted to teach in urban schools? These questions were the subject of my dissertation and my first book, analyzing research on urban teacher preparation over the past 30 years.

Reflecting on my own first months of city teaching, I realized that the conventional wisdom about what made city teaching so hard—that poor, minority kids were difficult to teach—couldn't explain my situation. I had been a confident teacher of poor, minority students in the suburban schools, so something else had brought on my difficulties at Julia Richman High School, my first job in the city schools. When I focused on the nuts and bolts of my first semester, I identified several aspects of school life that had caused me grief. I had been nervous about teaching in a school that was racially segregated, one in which teachers were White and the students minority, but I trusted that this would not be an insurmountable problem for me because I had learned how to work with students from many different backgrounds in my previous experience. In the suburbs, my classroom had been well organized but informal, and I had easily won the trust of my students. In the first months at Julia Richman, I had to figure out dozens of ways to get around regulations, procedures, and policies that kept me from being the kind of teacher I had been before.

As is the case in most schools, urban or suburban, at Julia Richman a new teacher was given the worst program. What makes this practice especially pernicious in city schools is that often teachers aren't hired until school has actually begun, so they have no time to prepare, not even a day. I had five remedial classes, mostly 9th graders, and no appropriate materials; an assignment to patrol the halls; a homeroom of

40-plus 9th graders; and three different classrooms, three floors apart. I was used to doing clerical work, but the volume and rigid specifications of the paperwork at Julia Richman overwhelmed me. Taking attendance was a painstaking task, requiring small cardboard strips called Delaney cards set into slotted folders, in addition to a roll book for keeping track of grades and attendance. I wasn't shy about asking questions, like how I could get chalk and paper or how photocopying was done, but finding someone to ask was a monumental challenge. The secretaries in the main office told me to ask my department head, who was nowhere to be found, and my colleagues were never free when I was. The assistant principal in charge of administration could occasionally be found in his office, but he let me know the second week that I was violating the appropriate chain of command by coming to him with questions and problems. In this school, finding out how to do the most basic tasks was a full-time job.

Homeroom, which began the day, was totally exhausting. I couldn't figure out how to treat the students humanely and still do my paperwork. Within a 15-minute period, teachers had to distribute and collect numerous forms as well as take attendance using two different methods: sorting computer cards for each student and recording attendance using special symbols in a binder. Learning the students' names and matching names with faces were themselves problems because attendance was very spotty. Many students were repeating 9th grade for the second, third, or fourth time; they visited homeroom and school only on the first of the month to receive their subway passes for free transportation. I had several 17-year-olds registered in my homeroom, and I learned that each term they were issued the same computer-generated program of courses they had failed the previous semester. I was their only contact with the school, and I saw them only for 15 minutes a month!

Other aspects of school life also disoriented me. Like many urban schools, Julia Richman was racially segregated. It had few African American or Spanish-speaking faculty, although the students were Black, Dominican, and Puerto Rican. Almost all of my own education and teaching had occurred in desegregated settings, and I was used to teaching amid racial tensions, but Julia Richman was a tinderbox. Though never publicly discussed, racial tensions—between Hispanic and African American students, between students and European American faculty—were physically palpable. Seemingly mundane disagreements immediately assumed racial dimensions. More than once I was called a "White bitch," and I commonly heard students hurl racist epithets at one another. Yet I was left on my own to figure out how I should navigate racial issues with students.

What abilities, knowledge, and attitudes helped me to overcome these barriers to successful teaching? When I analyzed my experience, I realized that my preparation to teach had been inadequate, but what rescued me was the ability to reflect on my teaching and improve it without assistance. In addition, when I began to blame the students for situations that were frustrating me, I stopped myself, refocusing on the conditions outside the classroom that were causing the problem. I looked for rational explanations for their behavior, and when I couldn't figure out plausible reasons on my own, I asked the students. For instance, I was overwhelmed by taking attendance because students constantly came late, yet the *worst* error a teacher could commit was to send the attendance binder down late after homeroom. The school's average daily attendance, taken during homeroom, determined its funding, and the administration communicated to teachers that the punctual reporting of every revenue-bearing body in the school that day was the teacher's most important responsibility. I felt caught between the demands of my job and the students' failure to do what they were supposed to do. A colleague told me to lock the door a few minutes after the late bell, to exclude latecomers. This forced students to walk down four flights of stairs after homeroom to the attendance office to correct the record; but it also made them late to their next class. Although I didn't feel right about locking the door, I tried it, in desperation. Students responded to this tactic by beating on the wooden door so violently the frame shook. Their rage showed me that my first impulse had been correct and that the strategy was inhumane, and I quickly dropped it. I should tell you, as a warning to prospective teachers who may think at this point that I should have maintained the "get-tough" strategy, that the door of the colleague who counseled me to lock out latecomers was set afire not long after she told me to imitate her.

As I struggled to devise a routine that permitted me to complete homeroom attendance on time, I asked students why they were late. Some had family obligations, like taking younger siblings to school; others worked until late at night and grabbed a few more minutes of sleep in the morning; but most complained that they depended on the subway and that the trains were notoriously unreliable. Subway trains came late, skipped stations, and were so overcrowded as to be unridable. I weighed the options: I couldn't do anything about their fatigue or family tasks, but I knew from my previous jobs that if I cajoled and applied friendly pressure, I could get a significant portion of these students into homeroom on time. On the other hand, the problem with the trains was new and formidable. I couldn't punish students for the Transit Authority's malfeasance, but on the other hand, I felt that I had to help them learn that if the subway couldn't be counted on, they had to leave home earlier. I asked students in homeroom for their suggestions and negotiated a method of taking attendance that satisfied us all: I sorted the computer cards but did not mark the attendance binder until the last 2 minutes of homeroom, allowing latecomers time to be marked present. At the bell heralding the end of homeroom, a student took the attendance binder to the office, and thereafter late students were obliged to go downstairs to change their record.

The alteration in the way I handled attendance seems so small and insignificant, yet it allowed me to use homeroom to get to know my students, to offer advice and encouragement. Homeroom changed from a trial to an opportunity to be with students in an atmosphere free of academic pressure. My successful adjustment to city teaching was a process of figuring out dozens of small changes like this one, which made me more comfortable and relaxed with my students and gave me breathing room to figure out how I could deal with the racial and social tensions in my classroom.

Since I've become a teacher educator who prepares prospective urban teachers, I've had to analyze how I can teach brand-new teachers to take on responsibilities that were difficult for me as a seasoned professional. The information in this book is a distillation of what I have learned from working with my students at New Jersey City University over many years and for a brief time at the College of Staten Island. Their questions, concerns, and insights have helped me to understand more clearly what new urban teachers need to know. In the process of trying to prepare prospective and beginning teachers, I tried to find a book that described school conditions realistically and offered ideas about how a new teacher could overcome the obstacles I had faced; finding none, I wrote the first edition of this book.

The recommendations I make to you about teaching are rooted in my own values, as a teacher and a citizen, just as your decisions about what and how to teach are framed by your beliefs, consciously acknowledged or not. You should, therefore, want to know more about my beliefs about education so that you can weigh the ideas I present against your own. In my role as a researcher and writer, I try to convince educators that we can't understand or change the way students and teachers act in urban schools unless we look at what's different about the urban school setting rather than examining decontextualized student and teacher characteristics. I discuss this in the next chapter as I explain how teaching in an urban school is different from teaching in other settings. Another idea that influences the recommendations I make is my belief that schooling is a vehicle of limited effectiveness for promoting equality because many factors that schools and teachers can't control directly—most importantly, the availability of jobs that pay a living wage and of quality social services—influence children's development. Although this book is not directly about life outside of urban schools, I think it's important that you understand my perspective because it influences the advice I give you. As you read this book, you should be thinking about how my values influence the decisions I've made and how your beliefs will shape your thinking about how to do your job.

My beliefs about education's social and political purposes and the teacher's role in schooling have also been central to the decisions I've made about how to relate to administrators, teachers, parents, and students. I'm committed to helping all students learn how to think critically and bring their own knowledge and beliefs to bear on making decisions that will shape their lives and our society. I think that the schools should be democratic institutions, in terms of their own practices and organization and in terms of the values they teach students. As a citizen and teacher, I'm opposed to schools being given the responsibility of ranking and sorting students for the job market.

My ideas about dealing with cultural differences in the classroom similarly reflect my values about cultural diversity in American society. I think that American society has shortchanged itself and immigrants and minorities by insisting that they reject their heritage and languages to become "real" Americans. The notion that we treat all people fairly when we treat them all the same is a fallacy, especially in education; it denies the histories of oppression and discrimination that influence how students respond to schooling and how schools still regard them. Teachers must be knowledgeable and mindful about the ways in which a child's membership in a social group may influence learning and school success. However, in the last analysis, the key category in teaching and learning is the individual. For this reason, I think that information about cultural differences is best understood as background material that may—or may not—be helpful with a particular student. Poor, minority parents and students can make sense of the disparity between their culture, their language and social customs, and the White, middle-class norms of schools in contradictory ways. Some may view the differences as a barrier to integration into American society; for others the differences are a strength, to be valued and sustained. I think that teachers should respect the right of parents and students to hold beliefs about assimilation and acculturation that differ from the stance of the school and the teacher. Our responsibility is to provide students and parents with the information and tools they need to make informed decisions, to give them access to the knowledge and attitudes that the powerful assume and acquire unconsciously. The choice of how they regard power relations in society, however, belongs to students and parents, not their teachers.

The point of view I've explained can be criticized for many reasons. Some researchers and educators may fault my perspective for being individualistic, in terms of both student achievement and teacher performance; others may argue that my thinking does not give data about cultural and racial distinctions the primacy they should have in our analyses of teaching and learning. Another argument I've encountered is that I slight the importance of the powerful forces of discrimination and oppression that teachers must counter and explicitly explain. Some educators disagree with my focus on what a teacher can accomplish in her classroom. They contend that the schools are set up to reproduce and justify existing inequalities and emphasize the relative powerlessness of individual teachers to reverse this situation.

I think it's possible for good city teachers to disagree about the political values and ideas I outline. However, what distinguishes urban teachers who thrive from teachers who do not is the ability and determination to win, retain, and deserve parents' and students' trust. I think that too much energy has been expended on trying to determine the single best way to teach rather than accepting that there are as many ways to organize classrooms and learning as there are talented, caring teachers and specific school contexts. Please don't misconstrue this to mean that "anything goes." Certain teaching strategies are clearly superior to others, for example, for communicating information, teaching high-level cognition, reducing interethnic tensions, or nurturing creativity. But I'm always interested to observe how some people successfully use techniques that I can't, and vice versa. Rather than demanding that all schools and classrooms look the same, we need to try to understand why contradictory theories of learning can yield instructional strategies that work well with different children and teachers.

Although you need to learn to adapt to the school setting, you should keep in mind that school conditions like overregulation and lack of resources are not acts of providence or nature. Unlike the weather, these circumstances result from political and social decisions about schooling that can and should be changed. Until economic and social conditions outside the school are improved, until urban schools are funded adequately and transformed organizationally, individual teachers will fight a losing battle to reach all of their students. But it *is* a battle—for children's lives—one in which better-equipped and better-educated teachers will do a superior job. I think urban teachers should consider their jobs to be "holding actions" that can't compensate for the effects of class discrimination, racism, and sexism or for the political and social neglect of cities and poor, minority kids. Yet teachers' efforts to help kids whose only chance of economic mobility is an academic credential affirm the possibility of increased opportunity. I view teachers' struggles to help city kids acquire dreams and achieve them as important moral and political acts.

When teaching is the wonderfully satisfying, intellectually absorbing activity that it can be, most questions that arise are too complex to be answered with formulas. If teaching decisions really take into account the neighborhood, students' personalities and needs, and school culture, no one can give you formulas about how to teach or handle a particular kind of problem. Therefore, this book will not give you recipes to follow—steps to follow in careful order—to produce fine urban teaching. Instead, I try to provide you with frank, accurate information about and analysis of urban school systems and advice about situations that are likely to be troublesome.

This book contains no footnotes, endnotes, or bibliography because I want it to be conversational, and in normal discussions people don't generally give sources to back up their ideas or to let you know the origin of a thought. But please don't misconstrue the absence of traditional references to imply that I've written this book without reading a great deal and thinking about other people's ideas. As I explain in a later section, you will have to take personal responsibility for your own intellectual and professional growth because most urban schools don't provide much help that you'll find useful. As a teacher I maintained an active involvement in professional organizations and read as much as I could. Although my recommendations are my own in the sense that I offer them, my thinking has been influenced by countless writers and researchers.

The most difficult aspect of writing this book was keeping in mind that I am writing for many different kinds of people who are prospective and beginning teachers. Some of you fit the description of the traditional teacher candidate: a single, monolingual female from a lower-middle-class or working-class family, raised in a suburb or small town. Others are mature, change-of-career students or women returning to college after sending their children off to school. Maybe you are a recent graduate from an elite university and have taken a job as a city teacher through one of the many "alternate route" programs developed in the past few years. Some of you are members of groups that have historically not been well served by urban schools: African Americans, Puerto Ricans, Chicanos, Native Americans. Maybe you have emigrated from another country or, though born in this country, identify closely with the culture and language of another nation.

I've observed in my own personal history and in the experiences of most of the student teachers and first-year teachers with whom I've worked that the key task in the first plunge of having your own classroom is developing a clear sense of identity. You need to figure out who you want to be when you are the teacher, to create an identity as a teacher that is consistent with your personality, values, and beliefs.

In my last year of teaching high school, a student teacher I'll call Rebecca Stokes, who was enrolled in the teacher preparation program in a nearby university, took over two of my classes. Rebecca floundered much of the semester; we had countless conferences, and I made many suggestions about planning lessons and teaching, yet she seemed not to grasp them. Finally, at midterm, she admitted to me that she was still grappling with what it meant for her to be the teacher. She still had great difficulty being called "Miss Stokes" by her students and confided that up until this point in her life the only people who had ever called her "Miss Stokes" were the secretaries in doctors' offices. Who was this mysterious "Miss Stokes" who had the power to call parents, give grades, and pass judgment on students' work? By the end of the semester Rebecca had acquired a sense of who she was and wanted to be as a teacher of English, and the students were sad at her departure, as she was, too. However, the process was difficult, even painful, and required honest, serious thinking about her reasons for becoming a teacher.

Who do you want to be as a teacher? For some prospective and beginning teachers, like Rebecca Stokes, being addressed as an adult with authority over others feels odd. Some new teachers, especially those who are recent college graduates and have always met with academic and personal success, face in their first weeks and months of city teaching a new, bitter reality and view of themselves: They are not excelling. For other new teachers, those who have already experienced many adult responsibilities that require the exercise of authority—like raising children or having a career—acquiring an identity as a teacher is usually less difficult because they are acquiring a new occupational identity rather than learning what is involved in taking on the responsibility of a job. However, more mature students often feel anxious about becoming the "Mr. Brown" who directs a group of 1st graders rather than the one who sells books because they are making a significant change in their lives. The stakes feel much higher in this new occupation because the old sense of self has been put at risk. The process of acquiring an identity that fits you is intensely personal. It's a journey that you must make alone.

I hope this book will help you to critically examine your values and ideals about teaching. As I explain in Chapter 4, the greater the social distance between you and your students, the more essential it is for you to be clear about your own expectations and beliefs when you assume responsibility for a classroom of students. New and prospective teachers almost always worry more about class control than any other issue, and for good reason. We can't know in advance if we can handle a group of 30 young people in a room together because we've never tried. As I discuss in Chapter 6, your control stems from your moral authority; however, your moral presence depends on your having a clear sense of how you want your students to regard you and how you regard them in your capacity as the classroom leader. Nothing about urban teaching contradicts the tenets of good practice outside of city schools, but successful urban teaching requires more and better teaching skills and knowledge. I explain in Chapter 2 why the characteristics of urban school systems demand that urban teachers be better at what they do to achieve the same results as their colleagues in suburban schools.

If it's harder, why choose to be an urban teacher? Like much in life, it's a greater challenge, but the rewards are immeasurably larger, too. The culture in most schools (alas) rules out discussions of teaching's rewards, so there's little chance for teachers to share feelings of accomplishment with colleagues who appreciate how hard-won these victories are. (The last place you'd ever say that you enjoyed your class or did something wonderful would be the teachers' lounge!) But the accomplishments can be breathtaking—when we find the opportunity to examine them.

In part because teaching is considered "women's work," it is held in low regard in the dominant society. In fact, I'll admit that I was not particularly proud of being a teacher until I taught in city schools and realized education's importance—my importance—for my students. One spring, I was given an award as Teacher of the Year by the local Chamber of Commerce. I agreed to the honor, provided it was understood that I accepted it as a representative of the dozens of dedicated teachers in my school, Martin Luther King Jr. High School. In that capacity I attended a ceremony honoring other public employees receiving commendations. The reception was filled with local businesspeople and community activists, and I was at a loss about what to say in my acceptance speech. Right before I was scheduled to receive my award, a firefighter was extolled for an especially daring act of heroism in rescuing an elderly woman trapped in her burning apartment. He had saved a life. What had I done in comparison?

Then I recalled my encounter with Lydia a few weeks earlier. Lydia had been in my 9th-grade English class. She was older than the other students, and she did no homework, though her reading and writing skills were respectable. Her attendance was irregular, and she was moody; her relations with classmates were often strained. One morning she came into class and started crying. I gave her a bathroom pass so that she could compose herself, and when she returned I found a few minutes to talk with her in the hall while students were working on group projects. She explained that family problems were driving her out of her mother's home and that she was living with her grandmother a great distance from school. I helped her make an appointment with a counselor I knew was empathetic and knowledgeable, suggested some other options, put my arm around her to reassure her, and then returned to the classroom to work with other students.

After that term I didn't see Lydia again for a few years and had forgotten about our exchange . . . so many others like it occurred on a regular basis. One morning she walked into my room, smiling radiantly, to thank me for our talk. She told me I had helped her change her life: She had completed a high school equivalency degree and a job-training program that was paying her enough to save for college. She had enrolled in a community college for the next semester. She was vibrant and hopeful, her eyes luminous with possibility.

Without knowing it, I had rescued Lydia. My act was not dramatic, as the firefighter's had been, and it was not recognized by anyone but Lydia—not even by me until she returned to express her gratitude. But I had saved a life, and as I told the audience about Lydia, I felt a new, deep respect for the work city teachers do.

Why teach in urban schools? Because you will have the opportunity to help students who need your talent and abilities and dedication. Because you can help save lives while you learn an immeasurable amount about life, yourself, and teaching from your students, who can teach you more than you can imagine.

2

What's Different About Teaching in Urban Schools?

Although I was an experienced, mature, confident teacher who had enjoyed working with students labeled "disadvantaged" in three suburban school districts, my first semester teaching in a typical New York City comprehensive high school was a professional trauma. I felt inadequate and unprepared, and I despaired about my decision to teach in the city schools. However, by the end of the second term I had regained my self-confidence and I spent the next 8 years thriving as a teacher in New York City high schools.

When I looked for answers in research, I found that most scholarship couldn't explain why I had difficulty making the transition or why I was successful. Most research took as its starting point the idea that what made urban schools and urban teaching different was the characteristics of students, and much of the research pinpointed the culture of the students and their families as the cause of academic failure. This explanation contradicted my teaching experiences, because my problems in adjusting to city teaching were clearly *not* primarily due to the type of student in city schools. Earlier in my teaching career I had enjoyed working with poor, minority students in suburban high schools, but in the city I felt overwhelmed teaching students whom researchers regarded as the same as those I taught previously.

Distinguishing Characteristics of Urban Schools

After reading 30 years' worth of research on urban teacher preparation, comparing the scholarship to what I had learned in my years of working in urban schools, I decided that by using *inner-city* and *urban* to describe poor, minority students, educators have inadvertently encouraged confusion about what makes urban schools, and the preparation to teach in them, special.

Part of the confusion comes from the fact that cities have always had the greatest concentrations of poor, immigrant students and of children described at different times in the nation's history as "culturally deprived," "disadvantaged," or "at risk." However, the students are only one part of the explanation for what makes urban teaching different. Urban school systems have other traits that create special problems and challenges for teachers. In my second career, as a researcher and teacher educator, I've tried to refine our understanding of what makes urban teaching different.

First, there are structural and organizational factors, like the school system's size and the centrality of the school bureaucracy. Urban schools are run by bureaucracies and by design cut off from the communities they are supposed to serve. Since their creation a century ago, urban school systems have been under pressure to resolve political and religious tensions in the nation's social fabric. The school system had to appear to treat all groups fairly, and the method of organization that seemed to do this most effectively was an impersonal bureaucracy. Rules and regulations were put into effect to standardize educational practices and treat students anonymously. However, learning, by its very nature, is an intensely personal, individual matter, so teachers and students in urban schools are caught in a system that undercuts their efforts to allow individuals to learn in the ways that are best for them.

Another important condition that has existed since urban school systems were created is that they have been plagued by inadequate funding. Teachers and students in the nation's cities have consistently faced a scarcity of supplies, materials, and time. For instance, though overcrowding in city schools due to immigration grabs headlines now, the situation is not new: At the turn of the last century, city classrooms were so crowded that students sat two and three to a desk.

Historically, students in urban schools have been different in terms of ethnicity and religion from students in other locales, and urban school systems have had the responsibility of educating a tremendously diverse group of students. As was true in the past, city schools today educate a high proportion of immigrant students whose families have recently come to this country to escape political persecution or extreme economic hardship. In addition, public schools have finally been held legally responsible for serving racial minorities, who were not given equal access to public education until the 1960s, when the civil rights movement called the nation's attention to the injustice of segregation and racial discrimination. Students and parents from groups who have failed to "make it" in our society may view conflicts with schools and school people as evidence that despite the rhetoric of equal opportunity, schooling cannot help them to achieve the American Dream. Parents who value languages and traditions that differ from those of the dominant society may be apprehensive that adapting to the majority culture will mean losing connections with the community that has sustained them. Schools often respond defensively to parent and student criticism, reinforcing suspicions that minorities will not be permitted to use the schools for social mobility.

The characteristics of urban schools that I've identified can be found to a lesser extent in many other school districts. For instance, the largest cities are now surrounded by small, older suburban school systems that resemble city schools in their student population and problems of underfunding. I saw this when I worked in a suburban school district outside New York City, but I also had the opportunity to see that the district's small size meant that communication between district administrators and school-site staff was fairly easy and informal. When I wanted to find out whether a student was correctly placed in my class, I walked down the hall to ask the guidance counselor. If the record seemed inaccurate or incomplete, she'd call across the street to the junior high, where the counselor knew the student personally and could correct or confirm the written record. In New York City student records might be kept in three different offices or they might have been lost in the student's transition from another school. In all three suburban school districts I worked in before teaching in New York City, I was the exception in commuting from the city; many teachers lived in the district and the school's neighborhood. I could turn to them for information about the community or a family, to understand my students better. At Julia Richman, some students knew one another from their neighborhood, East Harlem, but almost no teachers lived above 96th Street, the geographical border between Hispanic East Harlem and the White Upper East Side. As a faculty we were socially isolated from our students' lives outside the classroom.

For any school system that receives significant federal or state assistance, as most do today, decisions about curriculum, instruction, and budget are constrained by reams of regulations. Since passage of the federal legislation called No Child Left Behind (NCLB), federal regulation of school life has increased dramatically—despite the very small amount of financial support that the federal government provides to the states for schools. But urban school systems have their own separate rules and regulations, on top of the federal and state requirements. The maze of bureaucratic regulation can influence every facet of school life, from the books you use to teach reading, to your placement in a school, to your freedom to open a classroom window more than 9 inches. The larger the school system, the larger and, in most cases, more dysfunctional or "sick" the bureaucracy is.

All over the country school districts are dealing with the reality of immigration, which has made once-homogeneous school districts culturally and linguistically diverse. However, cities continue to be the first places most immigrants settle, so urban schools educate the greatest proportion of new immigrants. Poor children live in rural areas and suburbs as well as cities, but I think the supports that help poor families cope with the problems that accompany extreme poverty are more severely strained in cities. The anonymity of city life further increases the responsibilities schools have for educating children who can be hungry, homeless, or vulnerable to violence in their neighborhoods.

I think we can understand what makes urban schools different if we move away from the idea of an either/or answer—*either* a school system is urban *or* it isn't. Another way to define *urban* is to think of urban-ness on a continuum, ranging from the largest cities (New York City and Los Angeles) on one pole to the least urban communities (small, wealthy suburbs populated almost entirely with European Americans) on the other. The extent to which a district can be considered urban depends on the configuration and concentration of the factors I've discussed. However, the size of the school system is the key characteristic because the larger the system, the more the bureaucracy intrudes on life in classrooms. Furthermore, in urban schools, teachers, students, and parents have less access to decision making and are more isolated from one another.

Within large urban school systems, conditions in schools vary as much as those in the neighborhoods they serve. In general, schools serving more prosperous, stable neighborhoods have fewer of the characteristics and problems we associate with urban schooling. Although teachers are saddled with the same regulations and policies throughout a school system, the hardships are buffered in schools enrolling students from more affluent families. Each school in a district may receive the same allocation per student for supplies and materials, but teachers who work in schools in middle-class neighborhoods can expect parents to subsidize the supply budget; teachers in high-poverty communities can't. In some respects urban schools that educate students from more middle-class homes are closer on the urban-ness continuum to their suburban counterparts than they are to city schools in the poorest neighborhoods, because the schools' capacity to provide intensive support is not as overburdened. When I describe conditions in urban schools, readers should keep in mind that urban schools often differ enormously from one another, depending on their placement on the urban-ness continuum, as well as their institutional histories.

Prescription for Success: Acquire the Ability to Reflect

How can you be sure that you will not become one of the urban teachers who let the demands of the job overwhelm them? If you didn't start your teaching career with some confidence that you're different from those fatigued, cynical teachers who race the students to the doorway at the end of the day, you'd be ready for retirement before beginning your first job!

But confidence that you're a different type of person is not enough to keep you from succumbing to the roadblocks set in your intended path of helping kids to learn, of making a difference in their lives. The best insurance you can acquire to maintain your idealism and improve your teaching ability is to learn how to reflect on your life as a teacher. The idea of reflective teaching comes from John Dewey, who wrote about reflection in teaching long before I was born. However, his framework in part explains why I was able to make the transition to city teaching despite my inadequate preparation in education courses: I was able to reflect on my practice and improve it, with no outside assistance.

When I start talking about theory in my education classes, I always see some students respond with a "Not again!" look. I think that as a nation we emphasize the practical and we're suspicious of the value of ideas and theory. That's why we use the phrase "It's academic!" when we describe something as irrelevant or useless. Other societies look to intellectuals and scholars to lead them, but in this country book learning is "only academic."

If you have this tendency to dismiss theory, let me try to convince you that having a framework to analyze how you will make decisions is critical because it helps you make your professional development *conscious. You* will be in charge of your own growth by having a method of measuring how and what you do in the classroom. Your development won't be hit-or-miss but, instead, systematic.

The ability to reflect is valuable for all teachers but it's essential for urban teachers, who are faced with morally and politically complex decisions yet have almost no institutional support or help in figuring out how they should behave. In fact, the schools that demand the most difficult moral decision making are generally the ones that provide the least assistance—in any realm. The model of reflective teaching helps you to clarify and articulate how your values influence your decisions about your life in school; it aids you in remaining alert to other perspectives that contradict your own. I'll explain how this works by referring to the crisis in homeroom I described in the previous chapter, to illustrate what each quality involves. However, my brief description of Dewey's ideas should serve only as your introduction to reflective teaching. I strongly recommend that you learn more about this way of thinking about your teaching.

Dewey explains that being reflective has three aspects: being wholehearted, open, and responsible. As I struggled to find a solution to homeroom, I demonstrated wholeheartedness. Other teachers adopted procedures for attendance that angered and alienated the students. A teacher whose classroom was next to mine advised me to simply lock the door at the late bell for homeroom. I tried her solution for a few days, but when the students screamed at me to open the door and beat on the door, I realized I had to look for other solutions. Wholeheartedness calls for teachers to seek ways to fulfill their obligations to their students. In other words, "If at first you don't succeed, try, try, try again." The word also connotes an enthusiasm for and dedication to your work with children, qualities that contradict the civil service mentality encouraged by the norms and culture of the school bureaucracy.

Students' moral radar quickly identifies teachers who lack wholeheartedness, and such teachers lose credibility and trust. Remember the fate of my colleague who encouraged me to lock the door? An especially angry student set fire to her door.

Dewey uses the term *responsibility* to mean intellectual consistency and the willingness to pursue ideas to their conclusion. Although teachers must be conscientious, as the term *responsible* is generally defined, Dewey explains *responsibility* as the ability to critically examine our beliefs and actions in light of the values we profess. In the case of homeroom, I could have solved the problem in other ways—for instance, by staying in homeroom past the late bell to mark attendance and then coming late to the class that followed homeroom. But I value punctuality and believe that teachers should model the habits they want their students to acquire. For this reason, I couldn't be consistent with my values as a teacher and come late to class every day. How could I tell students they had to be in class on time when I arrived late?

Being *open* played a role in my decision because I developed my solution by examining the problem from several perspectives and seeking solutions from many sources. By habit and temperament, I am punctual. I am one of those people who's almost always on time for appointments. My students did not share my regard for punctuality, which frustrated me, but it did not discount the need to understand the situation from their perspective. As I later found to be true almost every time I asked students to explain a problem, their explanation was reasonable.

They pointed out to me that unlike many of their friends, they were coming to school—albeit late. They had difficult commutes on the subway, and many had other responsibilities before school that made them late, like dressing and feeding younger siblings and walking them to school. They felt that their circumstances merited consideration and should be translated into a flexible method for taking attendance. Listening to the problem from the students' perspective convinced me to swallow my anger at their being late so that I could ask them to help me find an acceptable compromise.

In addition to the qualities of openness, wholeheartedness, and responsibility, urban teachers need to understand the way conditions outside classrooms influence the ways teachers and students act. Political, social, and economic circumstances in the school and the community (even the world!) affect our lives as teachers and the decisions we make. Researchers refer to this as the social context, and if you think about the concept you'll see that thoughtful teachers automatically take it into account. When 15 fire engines shriek past your classroom window, the social context of the school is influencing your teaching. Will you try to shout over the noise or pause until it subsides? Skillful urban teachers realize that circumstances outside the classroom must be taken into account when they decide how and what to teach. Will you insist that each student bring in a notebook and pencils the first week of school, even if there's a strong chance that parents or a guardian are unemployed? If you consider factors like this in your decision making, you are drawing on the social context of the classroom in the process.

Learning to teach in urban schools is not the same as learning to deal with racism in school and society. *All* teachers need to know how to examine their own cultural frame of reference and to understand how prejudice and social inequality are reflected and reproduced in schooling. Nonetheless, the ability to stand back from ideas and values that we hold strongly—often without knowing it—is most important for urban teachers because the conditions in which they teach *discourage* this way of thinking and operating. Because urban schools are isolated from communities, teachers are cut off from the knowledge parents can provide about their children and their lives outside school. When teachers lack this knowledge and are unable to analyze problems from a variety of perspectives, they frequently blame the students or their families when the kids fail to meet expectations of school people for behavior and conduct.

In my preparation to teach, no one explained that the social context was an important factor, but my involvement as a political activist—in the civil rights, peace, and women's movements—had made me aware of how outside forces influence our thinking. In addition, I had taught in starkly different settings, so I could see that many of the city's procedures and regulations created problems for students and teachers. My life experiences taught me the importance of the social context before I started to teach, but new teachers can acquire the ability to take factors outside their classroom into account if they develop the ability to reflect.

The idea of reflective teaching has its critics. Some educators argue that teachers don't have the time or energy to reflect because their work lives are totally occupied with other important tasks. Of necessity teachers make decisions mechanically, without conscious reflection, they assert. However, my education students disagree with this analysis of reflective teaching and decision making. They report that they make a semiconscious mental recording of a problem as it occurs in the classroom, and at a later time they review the episode they've recorded in their mind. Furthermore, after doing this for a while, they become more proficient and learn how to reflect as a difficult situation occurs.

Reflection does not necessarily produce satisfying solutions. In fact, in urban schools you are likely to encounter a vast number of problems that have no completely acceptable answers. I think urban teachers face more situations that have no satisfactory resolution because their work occurs in a setting fraught with contradiction. Teaching is meaningful for students and instructors only when it is personal and individual, but urban school systems are structured to make schools impersonal and the people in them anonymous. To be successful, teachers must deal with students as individuals, but urban schools were developed to treat everyone interchangeably. The bureaucratic conditions that so heavily influence life in schools make teachers feel like unskilled laborers who are easily replaced, yet the most effective teaching requires considerable personal responsibility. Urban teachers must be dedicated to their profession and the people they serve, yet the circumstances of their labor continually remind them that they are hired help.

This contradiction between students' needs and workplace demands makes urban teaching very special and very difficult. However, I think that the more clearly you understand how conditions in the school influence your life as a teacher, the better prepared you'll be to make decisions that you can live with and still be a respected, successful urban teacher.

3 Dealing with the Urban School System

In the previous chapter I described what makes urban school systems and teaching in them special. In the next several pages I'll explain how the characteristics of urban school systems influence your life as a teacher and suggest how you can deal with the hurdles created by the system.

The most deleterious effect of the characteristics I've discussed is that they promote your demoralization, making you feel that nothing you can do will help your students. Understanding the sources of your fatigue and frustration won't eliminate them as factors, but if you can accurately analyze the origins of your problems, you'll be better equipped to figure out solutions.

Let me draw an important distinction between two concepts that are frequently confused—acknowledging the causes of a problem and excusing it. I think it's correct to say that teachers and students fail to achieve what they could and should in many urban schools without accepting or rationalizing these failures. In two of the city schools I taught in, many kids did not receive a good education. Almost all the teachers worked very hard and wanted to help their students succeed academically, but the school and school system constantly undermined our efforts. When we managed to step back from the school procedures and regulations to examine them critically, we saw how circumstances outside the control of the students and staff caused obstacles that interfered with our helping all kids achieve their potential. However, teachers in urban schools almost never have a chance to analyze school problems together, let alone with parents' and students' insights. As a result, each teacher is on his or her own to figure out how taken-for-granted practices, policies, and rules are hindering achievement.

Saying that the school system creates roadblocks for teachers and students to fulfill their potential is very different from saying that children who are not learning what they should cannot learn. In every urban school system you can find some successful schools serving poor children whose families totter on the brink of disaster; in almost every urban school you'll find a few teachers who work successfully with children whom other teachers dismiss as impossible to teach. And you'll find some students that no one has been able to reach.

One of the most stressful aspects of teaching in urban schools is that you will not be able to give each child the full help she or he needs, although this must be your ideal. When teachers say that certain kinds of children are uneducable, they are expressing frustration and anger at their inability to teach successfully. Rather than saying, "I can't help this kid," they say, "This kid can't/won't learn." It's almost never so clear that a child can't learn, and in putting responsibility for academic failure on the student, teachers absolve themselves of any obligation to change their own practices or any of the factors in the school that impede their success in helping children learn what's expected.

When you begin to think that a student or a class is hopeless, you need to summon up the energy to examine the situation critically. Some of the students in my college classes assume that being "critical" means you are accusatory or hostile, so I should explain that when I suggest that teachers adopt a critical stance, I mean you should become self-consciously analytical, trying to view the situation from a range of perspectives, including those with which you disagree. One of the first targets for your analysis should be school and district regulations and commonly accepted practices. Almost every policy will have some effect on your classroom, and more frequently than not, a problem you're having is being created or exacerbated by some regulation or policy, though its role may not be immediately apparent. Often what you experience is not the foolishness of the regulation or the practice but student misbehavior.

Before teaching in New York City schools, I never had significant problems with students' misbehavior, but I found myself battling with my students in my first 2 years in the New York schools. After a while I saw a pattern in my problems: I was obliged to enforce policies that students (and many teachers) disliked. Many of the regulations made sense in the abstract, but they created tensions between students (or parents) and teachers.

For instance, teachers were supposed to enforce a city policy that called for students to put all outergarments in lockers. Virtually no students followed this regulation, which was apparent when they wore their expensive sheepskin and down jackets to class, no matter what the room's temperature. I nagged, begged, and fulminated, but they continued to wear their coats into the room for the entire class session. On occasion they carried their coats, but they had nowhere to put them because the coats took up a seat of their own and I rarely had empty seats in the class.

The students' behavior seemed entirely perverse to me until I asked an otherwise well-behaved student why she violated the policy. She gave me an "Are you crazy—or what?" look and responded that nobody "wrapped tight"—that is, sensible—would *ever* put *anything* of value in the lockers because they were broken into so easily and frequently. No coat would be secure in a locker, she replied, and her mother had worked too hard for the money that bought the sheepskin for her to let anyone steal it.

As you can see from this situation, the school demanded that teachers enforce a rule that made sense if students had safe places to put their possessions; but under the circumstances, the rule made students choose between obeying a regulation or safeguarding their property. Teachers were responsible for pressuring students to abide by this unreasonable rule, and if I failed to enforce the rule, I risked a reprimand from an administrator who did not see the situation as I did; if I tried to enforce the rule, I confronted my students' wrath and resistance.

In this situation, as in countless others, I had to find a method to skirt a regulation that kept me from treating my students humanely. The strategy I used over the years to figure out an appropriate response consisted of these steps:

1. I critically examined the problem, looking at it from the students', parents', and administration's point of view. I assumed that all three parties were doing what they thought best despite the contradictions in their viewpoints and assumptions. When I listened to students I frequently saw the problem in an entirely different light.

2. I thought about whose point of view was most consistent with my own values about education. I'd question myself about the purposes of schooling and my moral responsibilities as a teacher.

3. I asked a colleague I respected how she or he handled this particular situation, and why. I'd question the person about the same issues I'd thought about myself: Was this strategy really fair to the students? But I also asked whether the method was practical: Would I be able to defend this method if an administrator questioned its use?

When I followed these steps in the coats-in-class situation, I decided that the rule was intended to encourage an academic milieu. Some parents or administrators might believe that if I didn't enforce the rule, I was not teaching students about appropriate behavior in an academic setting. On the other hand, I sympathized with students who did not want to risk having their coats stolen and thought that the administration should first direct its attention to providing secure lockers for students. I decided that students deserved to feel that their possessions were secure in school.

A well-respected teacher who was also the head of the teachers' union in the school told me that she had all her students remove their coats and jam them into their seats. When administrators questioned her, she invited them to take over the class and convince the students to follow the policy. I borrowed her strategy and modified it: I told the students that I understood why they wore their coats and would investigate what the administration was doing to make the lockers secure. When an administrator walked by my room, spotted the bulging coats, and told me that the students would have to take them to their lockers, I explained that they had refused to do this because the lockers were broken into. Rather than generating a batch of referrals to the dean, I had brokered this compromise. Satisfied with my answer, the administrator continued his patrol of the corridor.

From my description, the process sounds straightforward, even simplistic. However, several factors make the strategy I've outlined for you quite difficult to implement in the real life of a city teacher. One aspect of teaching in city schools that makes critically analyzing any one issue difficult is that you'll have dozens of problems percolating simultaneously. Finding time and energy to examine any particular issue is a challenge. You have to accept that you're not going to be able to find solutions to every problem at once, so you need to establish your priorities. What's creating the greatest hardship? Tackle that predicament first. In my case, the coats problem had a relatively low priority, so I wasn't able to think it through for 3 years.

A more powerful influence on your behavior is that you and the kids are in the classroom together; the people who make the regulations aren't. So it's natural to focus on what the students should be doing differently and to become angry when they don't perform as you want. The school system's structure and regulations are the hidden offender, but unmasking their culpability takes considerable energy.

What happens frequently is that teachers blame students and parents for not doing what they're supposed to, for not caring about education; parents and students blame teachers for not doing what they're supposed to, for not caring about them. This occurs partly because parents, teachers, and students have no opportunity to collaborate or communicate. Each group feels frustrated, overworked, and unappreciated. And they are!

Another factor that makes the three-step process I outlined above difficult to carry out is that we all bring a cultural frame of reference to schools. When our own frame of reference is the same as the school's, we have no reason to question practices that others view quite differently. For instance, if you've been raised in a family that values punctuality, it's hard to understand why some students don't come to class or school on time. Because school norms also support punctuality, it's quite easy to think that caring about education means coming to school on time. Therefore, when kids are consistently late, you may conclude that their families don't care about them or their schooling, especially if the parents are poor and uneducated.

When I share my own experience as a parent with teachers in my college classes, they gasp, shocked to learn that when my daughter was in grade school she was 10 or 15 minutes late to school at least twice a week. Because my college classes meet at night, my daughter went to sleep before I came home two nights a week. Obviously I care a great deal about education, but I also valued having a block of time with my daughter each day before she went to school. My priority—having a relaxed breakfast with my daughter when she hadn't seen me for 24 hours—didn't mean that education is a trivial matter in our family. Yet if I were not known to be a professor of education, if I had little formal education, teachers would probably assume that my behavior showed a disregard for my daughter's academic success.

Because urban schools offer so little opportunity for teachers, parents, and students to discuss school practices together, teachers can easily lose sight of alternate perspectives and misconstrue student and parental actions. This dynamic often occurs when teachers have not had life experiences like those of the students and parents they serve. When school people have not endured poverty and racial discrimination themselves, their frustrations make them prey to stereotypes about minority kids. Too often teachers see only the deficits, not the strengths students bring to school. Rather than analyzing what the school and teachers can do differently to help poorly achieving students succeed, too many teachers say that "these kids" can't learn because "these families" don't care.

In most urban schools, teachers have more formal education than the parents of children in their classes. The teachers also differ from the students in their classrooms in their ethnicity and race. Although the implications of this disparity for kids' learning are important, the situation is not new. It has existed since urban school systems were created in the latter part of the 19th century, when industrialization and immigration caused enormous social changes in our society, including the rapid development of cities and their school systems. The first teachers in urban schools were often young, White, Protestant girls raised on farms. They often taught children of new immigrants, many of them Catholics, who faced discrimination because of their religion, language, and class. In time, young women from this first wave of immigrants, often Irish Catholic, became city teachers and in their classrooms faced children of newer immigrants, like southern Italians, Poles, Slovaks, and Jews from Eastern Europe, all of whom brought their native languages and cultures.

As my brief sketch of this history indicates, the problem of "culture clash" between city teachers and students is not new, but it still presents a challenge. Because middle-class teachers almost never live in the poorer neighborhoods from which their students are drawn, the teachers seldom have relationships with parents in which both parties are equals. Furthermore, if on some occasion in their lives teachers have not had social interaction as equals with adults who are poor and uneducated, they may feel uneasy or even angry when parents who have little formal education themselves make suggestions about their children's education.

Teachers often want to be considered as professionals, experts who know what's best for children. This idea of professionalism has value, but it also contains a dangerous element. Although teachers need to have specialized knowledge and skills that parents do not, most parents have a kind of knowledge of their children that teachers seldom can: Parents know who their children are outside school. Yet urban schools do not provide teachers access to parents' knowledge and perspectives and do not give parents access to the teacher's rationale for decisions. In most schools parents hear from teachers only when children need money or a form signed, or when they misbehave. So parent–teacher relations are distorted by impersonal, bureaucratic arrangements that invite misunderstandings and mutual finger-pointing.

How can you deal with this isolation? As you think through problems you face, you need to be mindful, always, that in your classroom you are cut off from information about your students' lives outside school. As you devise methods of learning about your students and their families, you'll discover their strengths as well as their weaknesses. In most instances, the best starting point in this process is your students themselves.

My advice here is the same I'd give to a teacher anywhere, because good teaching starts with knowledge of your students. The more you know about your students, the more effective you will be because you'll be able to find that lesson or project that will excite them, and you. The more you know about your students, the more you'll enjoy your work because *they* will be giving to *you*. When your classroom encourages students to share their ideas, to critically examine the knowledge and perspective each person brings to the classroom, diversity becomes an asset. You and your students function like anthropologists, learning about the beliefs and ideas people hold in unfamiliar neighborhoods and cultures; your students and families educate you and one another.

If you are alert to the necessity of connecting what you do in your classroom to your students' lives outside school, you'll find strategies that work for you in your specific school setting. I think my experience as an adviser to the school newspaper was invaluable in helping me to understand students as people. In the informal setting of a club, teachers and students become acquainted with one another through an activity that requires the teacher's expertise far more than her authority. The understanding and satisfaction you acquire when you work with kids outside of the classroom supports your ability to step back from your frustrations in your role as teacher so that you can examine classroom problems from other perspectives.

Another method of becoming connected with your students as people is to be active in local community organizations. As a college student in California, I helped the farm workers' union organize support for their grape boycott, and I continued this work in my first years of teaching. I didn't realize that it helped me professionally until an irate parent, Mrs. Martinez, came to school to complain about her son Frank's placement in a remedial reading class. Our school contained many students whose parents came from Mexico and spoke Spanish at home, yet we had no programs to help them with the demands of regular English classes, other than placement in remedial reading. My colleagues warned me that Chicano parents could be very hostile about this problem, and they dreaded conferences of this sort. Sure enough, Mrs. Martinez displayed her anger even before our meeting began, waving away my effort to

introduce myself. Then she noticed the "Boycott grapes" pin that I habitu-
ally wore, and her demeanor changed instantly. She asked if I worked
with the union, and we briefly discussed the boycott effort. She and Frank
often picketed in front of local supermarkets, and I distributed leaflets at a
market near my home. After this exchange, Mrs. Martinez and I were able
to work out a less-than-satisfactory solution for Frank, but one that made
us allies in trying to change the school's offerings and in helping Frank.
Our adversarial relationship changed to an alliance.

If you have not had considerable experience working with city kids,
you need to become comfortable being with the kinds of children you'll
be teaching, preferably before you put yourself in a position of authority. Learning how to exercise authority is almost always difficult for new
teachers, and cultural confusion and ignorance exacerbate an already
stressful task. In urban schools you simply aren't given opportunities to
know your students as people, so you have to bring your own knowledge of their life circumstances to the classroom and become comfortable working with them on your own.

Once you're fairly confident that you'll be relaxed working with city
kids, the most efficient method of preparing yourself to face the challenges I've described is to student-teach in a school that's similar to the
one where you think you'll have your first job. Many of the jobs for new
city teachers are in schools that are the most difficult to teach in, and
your practice teaching will be most beneficial if you work in a setting
that approximates the conditions you'll find yourself in with your first
job. Your cooperating teacher will be able to give you many of the practical suggestions for dealing with school policies and rules that you'll be
in desperate need of during your first years.

What if you attended a racially segregated school or an urban school
that allowed a high proportion of students to fail? Then you already
know what such schools are like and won't need a great deal of help
in becoming comfortable. In fact, you may be *too* comfortable. For this
reason, I urge you to student-teach in an integrated school that helps
all kids to achieve academically. One student teacher I supervised—a
remarkably mature, young African American woman who had attended
all-Black urban schools that failed many students—told me that her eyes
were opened when she completed the first phase of her student teaching in a well-regarded suburban school. She was struck by the excellent
facilities and instructional techniques that could have been used, but
weren't, by her own teachers, and by the mutually respectful relations
between teachers and students. If you've already experienced the irra-

tionality of a school bureaucracy and know firsthand how urban schools can fail their students, use your student teaching to experience school environments that make you mindful of new possibilities.

I know that student teaching is a great financial hardship on most prospective teachers, and many want to find ways to circumvent the requirement. If teaching had the respect it deserves, with financial support from the government, urban school systems would fund paid internships for people who showed they were responsible and knowledgeable enough about teaching to take on classroom responsibilities. We would have student teaching—with a salary. The present reality is that few of these paid internships exist. Instead, "alternate-route" or "fast-track" programs have been created for people who want to try teaching but avoid the time-consuming coursework and the unpaid labor of student teaching. In general, teachers recruited through alternate-route and fast-track programs for city school systems teach in schools that are difficult to staff because the neighborhoods are dangerous or the schools are poorly run—or both. Alternate-route candidates are also sought after for "shortage areas," like math, science, bilingual education, and special education.

My phone rings off the hook with people who ask me about whether they should bite the bullet and enroll in a traditional program or go the alternate route. Before making the decision, you need to reflect on why these jobs are available to people who have no formal preparation to teach. After all, if you had a choice, would you go to a new lawyer who had passed the bar exam but bypassed law school?

One rationale for alternate-route programs is that they attract candidates with qualities that traditional teacher candidates often lack, perhaps shared life experiences with students in the communities in which they will be teaching, or significant work experience in a field in which an academic subject is used, or impressive academic credentials that include a degree from an elite college or university. Wealthy suburban schools on occasion hire new teachers for these same reasons. I know several people who did doctoral work in prestigious universities and were offered and accepted jobs in K–12 schools, teaching their subjects with no formal preparation in teaching. They made the adjustment well and have enjoyed their careers.

Urban school systems do not generally hire alternate-route candidates because they prefer them but rather because they cannot find enough traditionally trained teachers to fill positions. There are no teacher shortages in any subject in the most prosperous suburban school districts, which are swamped by applicants when they advertise an opening, even in special education or bilingual instruction. In a nutshell, shortages in schools exist because people don't want the jobs, and teachers who have other job options take those other positions. If you take a job in a hard-to-staff school, you need to realize that you are taking a position other people don't want, often for reasons that you will share.

We have lots of evidence that well-run alternate-route programs can successfully recruit, educate, and put into city schools the high-quality teachers that children need and deserve. These programs are especially good at attracting and preparing minority career-change adults who work well with kids and can be fine teachers but can't afford to forgo their salaries to do student teaching. Unfortunately, alternate-route programs vary widely in their quality. Some screen candidates well and work closely with school districts to give their recruits teaching positions in which novices will have the support of administrators and colleagues who are truly mentors. However, I am sad to say that from what I've seen and read, it seems most alternate-route programs do *not* adequately prepare and support the people they recruit.

Another significant problem is that the "quickie" certification programs often require getting a master's degree in the first few years that you teach. Often the programs pay for some or all of your graduate work, as long as you continue to teach. It sounds like a great deal! Be aware that there are problems that are not easy to spot before you sign up. For one, there's often a big disjuncture between the coursework that's required for the degree and what struggling new teachers feel they need from an education class. Often the college coursework seems too theoretical, unconnected to immediate crises new teachers face in the classroom. The professor may assign readings about principles of child development while you want to know how to get the kids to stop talking. Plus, you're writing those research papers when you need to be planning your classes.

A well-thought-out program of teacher education that prepares you to gradually assume your responsibility as a teacher can make your first years of teaching less stressful and more rewarding. In deciding whether an alternate-route program is really a bargain, consider the price you are willing to pay for your psychological well-being in your first 2 or 3 years of teaching. Even with solid preparation, you can count on your first year of teaching to be tough. If you become a city teacher through an alternate-route program, you should expect a first year that is enormously difficult because your learning will come from trial and error. I have seen more than a few people who have acquired their classrooms through fast-track programs stunned by the enormity of the challenges they face. One young woman told me she felt like a deer blinded by headlights. Often they've been successful in everything they've done in life and did not imagine that they would meet so many problems that they could not solve. They never anticipated that teaching would be so hard and can't understand why they can't take charge of 34 kids in a 7th-grade math class. What could be so hard about that? Plenty—as they soon learn!

Consider how your preparation will influence the kids whom you teach. They are captive inhabitants of the environment you create in your classroom. I know the advice that follows may sound unfeeling on my part, but I must pose this situation from the point of view of kids whose families are counting on school achievement to improve their children's life prospects. Sometimes new teachers who are very miserable in their first weeks of teaching just walk away from the job. The teacher's departure often sets in motion a process called "churning." No replacement lasts long because the class is so difficult, and with the subsequent exodus of each new teacher, the class becomes increasingly unruly. If the school is in an impoverished neighborhood or does not have a great reputation, there is little chance the principal can hire a certified teacher. Often long-term substitutes are used so that the class is at least "covered." And so the academic year is lost for the kids whose teacher left. This cycle was tragic when I was teaching high school and is more so now because the schools put so much more pressure on kids to achieve academically and yet provide fewer options for those who (through no fault of their own) have not been given the instruction they need to pass standardized tests or be promoted.

Sometimes alternate-route teachers endure a very stressful first year but do a respectable job and go on to have productive teaching careers. I think their success stems from personal attributes and also from the quality of their programs, but sometimes they've survived due to sheer luck, like having a colleague or principal with whom they "clicked." The reasons a person may do well in a fast-track program are often due to life experience, like knowing how to navigate in a bureaucracy or being resilient in the face of great disappointment. Consider this in your decision.

What about substitute teaching? Isn't that sufficient classroom experience so that you don't need to *pay* the college to work as a teacher? Absolutely not! Working as a substitute gives you practice in controlling a class, not teaching. In important ways it's very poor preparation because it miseducates prospective teachers about the relationship between lesson planning and classroom management. Substitutes must establish themselves as the authority but do not determine the intellectual content or social environment of the classroom. In a teacher's day-to-day relations with students, high-quality instruction is the key to creating a productive classroom.

Almost all the advice I've given in this chapter would also apply to a lesser degree to suburban schools that have many of the characteristics of urban school systems. However, the difference is in the degree. City schools don't allow much margin for error; you and your students pay a high price for your mistakes because the system provides few or no safety nets. If you handle a confrontation with a teenager poorly, he or she may not return to school for the entire semester, and no one in the school will follow up on the absences since guidance counselors typically have caseloads of several hundred students. If you don't follow up on a student who's sleeping in your class to find out the reason and help as best you can, no one else will.

Regardless of how you arrive at your first teaching job in a city school, I hope you will think about your moral obligations should you find that the job is not what you anticipated. Once you take on the challenge of having your own classroom, it comes with responsibility to the kids assigned to you. It may seem that no one will care if you don't remain for the entire year, but I assure you the kids will miss you, terribly. So if you are reading this book while struggling in your first year, I hope you will remain until June at least. Do recall that even as an experienced, confident teacher I questioned my ability in my first months in a city high school.

The responsibility is daunting, even overwhelming. In the next chapters I provide you with detailed advice to help you do your job as well as you can. Keep reading!

4 The Urban School Setting

In the previous chapters I've described in general terms what makes teaching in urban schools different from teaching in other settings. For the next several pages I'll discuss how these factors influence your relations with colleagues and your responsibilities as a new teacher. I think this information will help prepare you for the many frustrating situations you'll confront as you begin your career.

Sociologists describe bureaucracies that aren't functioning as they should as "sick." For example, when a bureaucracy is sick, the various units work at cross-purposes; administrators are likely to be either compulsive rule-followers or scofflaws. Unless you've tangled before with a sick bureaucracy, you probably won't appreciate how much of your workday is influenced by bureaucratic intrusions. Even when your classroom door is closed, regulations and mandates influence your work, as do seemingly irrational, foolish, and self-defeating procedures you are told to follow. In fact, the foul-ups begin even *before* you've started to teach!

Your First Job

For new teachers, the first years are almost always stressful because you have too much to learn. Researchers have found that even when you have had solid preparation, you're likely to struggle with a very steep learning curve your first year, operating on automatic pilot. By your second year, you'll be able to recall ideas you learned in your preparation to teach and apply them.

The budget for the academic year that begins in September, which often isn't given to principals until after school ends in June, determines the number of teachers a school receives and therefore each person's teaching assignment. Urban schools generally hire and assign teachers to classes much later than do prosperous suburbs, sometimes on the first or second day after the term has begun, sometimes even later. Federal regulations stipulating the requirements for a teacher to be "highly qualified" have created pressure on urban school systems to make sure teachers

meet the standard set in the law, so there is even more juggling of teachers' assignments than there was previously. In schools that are fairly well
functioning, the law has diminished the problem of your being hired to
teach a subject in which you have no academic background, a problem in
areas that have severe shortages, like math and science. However, urban
school systems have also found ways to circumvent the requirements, and
if you are considering taking a job in an area for which you have little or
no academic preparation, you'll want to think about the questions I pose
in Chapter 3 about alternate-route and fast-track programs.

A rational person would expect formal support systems to assist
teachers new to the profession or the school, especially in schools that
serve students with the greatest needs. This is almost never the case in
urban schools. In general, the worse the teaching conditions, the less
authentic assistance you'll receive. In most urban schools, new teachers
are left to fend for themselves. They are usually observed by administrators because these formal observations are required by law, but the
observations are generally pro forma. Rarely does a supervisor have the
time to assist new teachers with their eminently reasonable questions
and concerns. In the most dysfunctional schools, administrators are so
overextended that they may never observe new teachers if they trust
that they are competent—and perhaps even if they do not. I was not
observed my first year of teaching in New York, and a former student
teacher of mine who works in an urban school system under state re-
ceivership confided that in 2 years of teaching, *no one* had observed
him teach. He had received absolutely no feedback, positive or negative, about his teaching from another adult.

In the past, this lack of supervision created a fairly common set of
circumstances that some wonderfully creative teachers exploited: For
their first jobs, they were assigned to teach in poorly functioning schools
but chose to remain when they might have transferred elsewhere because they were free from administrative intrusions. The other side of
this coin was that they worked in a school that allowed pretty horrible
abuses of many sorts, precisely because there was no oversight. The
growing pressure from standardized testing has altered this situation
because teachers may still not have their classrooms observed by overextended supervisors, but their students' test scores are closely scrutinized. This change has raised the stakes for new teachers, making my
advice about how to deal with testing (Chapter 6) more pertinent to
surviving in a school in which you lack basic support from a mentor
or administrator. The struggle for professional survival in these schools
is Darwinian: If you can't be entirely self-sufficient in learning how to

teach under extremely difficult circumstances, you probably won't endure with your idealism unimpaired.

Many urban school systems insist that new teachers attend district-wide programs for professional development during their first semester or two. The quality and scope of these programs vary widely, but you can probably count on receiving important nuts-and-bolts information about school rules and regulations. However, most urban schools offer no comprehensive training or support for new teachers. Many states require mentoring programs for new teachers; but more often than not in urban schools, little mentoring of substance occurs if the program does not contain funding for a reduced teaching load for both the mentor and new teacher, allowing them time to collaborate. If both teach a regular schedule, they have no time to look at each other teaching and discuss their mutual observations. Another limitation to these programs is that they frequently do not provide experienced teachers who want to become mentors with appropriate training, so although effective teachers are selected as mentors, they aren't skilled in analyzing or conveying information about their strengths.

Unless you're in a highly unusual school, your professional development will be in your own hands. I strongly recommend that if you've had formal preparation to teach, you think about giving yourself a year to become situated; your work as a teacher may be so overwhelming you won't have the time or energy to spare for graduate courses. The other advantage to waiting a year or two before you enroll in a graduate program is that your teaching experiences will help you focus on particular areas that need strengthening; another possibility is that after a few years of teaching you'll decide that you want to move into another kind of teaching or school work. If your teaching situation requires that you have an advanced degree within a time limit that precludes taking off time from graduate study, you'll have to bite the bullet and juggle teaching and graduate work for those first 2 years. My only advice is that you try to anticipate how grueling this combination of teaching and graduate study will be and clear your schedule of any personal business that can be delayed. More than one of my students has regretted scheduling a wedding in his or her first year of teaching.

Your Relations with Colleagues

Every school, urban or nonurban, has a different culture, and the culture affects your relations with colleagues. In some schools, especially those with a stable staff, teachers have traditions of sharing resources and celebrating important events. They may have close personal relations with one another—or longstanding feuds. In other schools the staff is quite atomized; holidays pass with only the most perfunctory acknowledgment, and everyone hoards materials.

Despite these differences, urban schools do have certain similarities in their culture that influence your relationships with colleagues. In larger schools, relations are more impersonal, and teachers may not even know the names of all the staff, especially if the school is departmentalized. In smaller schools, the staff is generally more closely knit. In *all* urban schools, teachers have far more to do than they can accomplish; time is an extraordinarily scarce commodity.

I suggest that from day one you turn your radar on, scouting the school for colleagues who can assist you. You probably won't find one person to help you with everything because no one will have the time. Instead, look for different colleagues to help you with various concerns. You don't need the most dedicated, inventive teacher to tell you how to get chalk, so ask the person whose classroom is next door. On the other hand, if you have a question or concern about how to handle a problem with a student, ask a colleague who seems to enjoy the students, one who talks respectfully to and about them.

I've never taught in a school, urban or suburban, in which staff members freely discussed issues of race and class with one another. Racial tensions are almost always a factor in schools, but they're almost never addressed. Because our society is so segregated, most of us don't discuss race in integrated settings, and schools don't provide opportunities for teachers—or students—to develop the skills and knowledge needed to examine hot issues, like race, with civility.

In Chapter 6 I suggest how you can establish positive relationships with your students, but here I should note that if you are European American and your students are not, you will benefit from the perspective that minority teachers can give you about the school and the students. For the same reasons, if your students are learning English, colleagues who share the same linguistic and cultural background can often be an invaluable resource. Remember that the school will not provide you with information about your students' lives outside school, so you'll have to find out for yourself who they are as people and how their families and community influence their schoolwork.

For instance, as an English teacher I was struck by the enormous difficulty some of my students who were native speakers of Spanish were having in their writing, in comparison to others who were also Spanish speakers. I cornered a bilingual teacher well regarded by the students for possible explanations, and she informed me that Spanish-speaking students in the school came from two groups: Puerto Rican students who had lived in rural areas where free, compulsory public education effectively ended before middle school, and South American immigrants, primarily from Colombia and Ecuador, who had lived in cities and were children of relatively well-educated parents. The South American students had learned how to write fairly well in Spanish before coming to this country, so in my class they were able to build on the literacy skills they had developed in Spanish. The students from villages in Puerto Rico were learning how to write while they were learning English. This data helped me reformulate my instruction so that I was more effective with both groups of students, but I might never have understood the differences had I not sought advice from my colleague.

Establishing a professional relationship with a colleague who can be a "cultural informant" often isn't easy. Bilingual programs are administratively separate in most schools, so you'll have to be proactive to identify teachers who can help you. In addition, the African American teachers who are considered the best by students, parents, and administrators often devote themselves to helping their students directly and aren't active in school activities that attract other teachers, so you'll have to take the initiative to seek them out. You should do so because you can learn a great deal from the way they work with students as well as from the way they view the school. As a White teacher, I couldn't be the same with students as the Black and Hispanic teachers I respected; but I learned from their perspective and could adopt some of their techniques.

When I taught on Long Island, I was fortunate to team-teach with a wonderful male African American teacher who was beloved by the students. I could never *be* him, but during our year together I picked up methods of dealing with students that were more effective than the ones I had been using. For instance, he constantly reaffirmed his confidence in them, even when correcting behavior. He would often remind them that their behavior was not consistent with what their mothers had taught them, and he would put misbehavior in personal terms, telling students who were chatting during a classmate's recitation, "You're being rude," rather than saying—as I did—"You need to stop talking!"

Don't be afraid of seeming ignorant or foolish by asking questions, even if your colleagues seem harried and give you short answers. In my experience, although city teachers are very overworked, most recall how difficult their own first years on the job were and are willing to help newcomers as best they can.

Colleagues who are just as important to your survival are nonteaching staff. You should take the time during the first few weeks of school to become acquainted with these people who work in the school, especially security guards, secretaries, and janitors. They usually know more about the school's operations than anyone else. However, they're busy, too! Anticipate asking lots of questions, but don't expect a mentor.

I'm sad to acknowledge that in more schools than not—everywhere, not just cities—the discussion in the teachers' lounge tends to be negative; positive comments about teaching seem out of place. Unfortunately, especially for new teachers, it's the last place to go for help in planning lessons because that's not what's done in the lounge. Moreover, schools that have a dissatisfied staff usually have a teachers' lounge that exudes demoralization. In general, this is not a great place for you to spend your time out of the classroom if you want to retain your idealism. I do, though, know some excellent teachers who spend their free period in the teachers' lounge, using the time to chat about their personal lives and refueling psychically. Frankly, I don't understand how they do it. Perhaps you'll be able to filter out the negative, but don't think that you need to bond in the lounge to be respected by your colleagues.

I have tremendous respect for most city teachers, whom I've found to be conscientious and hard-working. However, because the conditions are demoralizing and the school is insulated from parents, even teachers who care about doing their job well may make inappropriate comments about students. Unfortunately, in most schools teachers do not publicly criticize teaching behaviors they consider wrong. That's also part of the culture of schools, and not just in cities.

When I heard colleagues insult students in ways I felt were morally wrong and racist, I didn't know how to respond without sounding self-righteous, so I held my tongue but felt that my silence made me complicitous. After a few years, I formulated a rejoinder that sounded just right for me, and I've used it successfully many times. When a frustrated, unhappy social studies teacher said to me "These kids are animals; they need zookeepers, not teachers," I replied, "Marvin, I know you don't believe that and so you shouldn't say it." Marvin stiffened a minute and then said something like, "There was a time I never would have said that, but the fact that I say it shows how burned out I am." On the other occasions when I said, "I don't think you really believe that," my colleagues showed momentary surprise but quickly agreed with me that the remark didn't convey how they really felt about their students.

Unless you teach in an exceptional urban school, you will probably hear about teaching practices that are indefensible, like teachers who hurl insults at students who misbehave, calling them "stupid" or "animals." My thinking about this problem is disputed by people I admire and respect, but I did not engage in personal confrontations with colleagues. For example, I never told colleagues that I thought something they said or did was racist or sexist because I felt that to do so would signal that I stood in judgment and would make further collaboration extremely difficult. Remember the distinction I drew earlier between explaining and justifying student behavior that is wrong? I think this differentiation applies to teachers' performance, too. Although teachers have more power than students—and therefore must assume more responsibility for what occurs in the classroom—they, like their students, are influenced by conditions in the school and the school system. Many teachers are angry and frustrated about the way they are treated by the school system. They feel under attack and unappreciated, insulted by rules and regulations that undermine their self-respect and authority. They sometimes vent their frustration on their students, which is totally indefensible; but in my experience, most teachers know when they do this that their behavior is wrong. I think they need to be reminded of their better inclinations, reminded about the ideals that inspired them to become teachers.

I want to draw a distinction between actually *seeing* teachers do things that are morally indefensible or illegal and hearing colleagues *say* things that are offensive. A student teacher I was supervising for my college, who taught a 3rd-grade class, informed me that she saw her co-operating teacher, in an isolated hallway, smack a misbehaving student hard on the head while scolding him for misbehavior. I reassured the student teacher that she would be protected against any recriminations but that I had to act, immediately, to inform my own supervisor at the college and set in motion its intervention. Anyone who sees kids being abused is bound, by law and professional norms, to report the situation to the proper authority.

Remember that seeing something with your own eyes and hearing secondhand about teachers' misconduct toward students are two different matters. The stories you hear may not be true. Still, I think that even as a new teacher you should convey to a respected colleague any information you hear about serious harm that is being done to a student. When I was teaching at a city high school, a female student confided to me that a male teacher was having a liaison with her friend. Worried, I asked the head of the teachers' union how the situation should be handled. We agreed that the union leader would pursue the issue with the teacher, warning him that if the student's story was accurate, the teacher's actions were a betrayal of professional norms and illegal. When I heard that the teacher was having a sexual relationship with yet another student, I reported what I knew to the principal.

As I hope my discussion makes clear, the misbehavior of your colleagues raises complex problems, especially for new teachers. We should be able to expect that egregious violations of kids' rights will be dealt with in a fair but swift fashion by administrators, but this is often not the case. In the situation in which the student teacher informed me that she had seen another teacher hitting a student, the principal intervened and informed the teacher she would be reported to child protection agencies if she repeated her behavior. But I learned subsequently that people in the school building had seen this teacher hitting students on other occasions and had informed the principal. Nothing was done. Perhaps it took my report to the college, which is an "outside" presence, to propel the administrator to act. Similarly, the teacher whom I reported to my principal had been identified as having liaisons with female students before. Yet the principal, an administrator who was quite caring toward the students, did not (to my knowledge) report the teacher to school authorities. Both situations illustrate how the tremendous insularity of schools allows breaches of the most basic professional norms. As a new teacher, you have an obligation to report to authorities anything you see that constitutes abuse. Your decision about how to deal with a colleague's behavior that falls short of abuse is complex and has to be based on many factors, including how effective your intervention will be in halting the behavior, how your actions will affect your ability to work with this person, and how your intervention will influence your relations with other teachers, students, and parents.

Often new teachers are angry at what they perceive as malfeasance on the part of more experienced colleagues. I understand the hostility that new teachers can experience toward faculty that they and administrators perceive as "dead wood." But I have a different way of viewing the situation that may help you to be more understanding about those colleagues you think aren't pulling their load. First, consider how you might regard your job if you had been teaching for 15 or 20 years. The teacher who

tells you that you've made a terrible mistake in becoming a teacher probably started off his or her career with ideals not too different from your
own. Very few people *begin* to teach with a negative attitude, so something happens to them after a while. At the start of your life as a teacher,
dwelling on those factors that demoralize your colleagues is counterpro-
ductive, but you should recognize them. Another way of thinking about
the demoralization and negativity that teachers project is that there's no
way to know for sure how these people act in their classrooms. Because
the school structure makes collaboration among faculty very taxing, urban teachers usually see one another in the worst light, as they complain
or compete for scarce resources. You don't see firsthand what your colleagues do in their classrooms all day; you only hear descriptions.

Sometimes a teacher who has only the harshest criticisms of her students will devote her time and money to sponsor a club or work with a
community group. I have observed the inaccuracy of my judgment of a
colleague's dedication when I changed my own routine or talked with
a faculty member who knew something that I didn't. In more than one
instance I learned that a colleague who was a less-than-ideal instruc-
tor sponsored an extracurricular activity that regularly detained him at
school until nighttime. On other occasions I'd see behavior that didn't fit
the negative conception of the teacher I had developed. One time, I left
school later than usual on a Friday and saw Mrs. M, a science teacher
whom students complained about all the time, departing the building on
a Friday afternoon with two armloads of papers she was taking home
to correct. Whenever I saw Mrs. M, she bemoaned our students' abilities
and lack of motivation. I had heard students calling her a "bitch" who
didn't care whether they learned her subject. She was one of the teachers who'd tell students, "I get paid the same whether you learn this or
not." Yet here was Mrs. M, overloaded with papers that would occupy
her weekend, trying to help her students pass the state exam in science.
That's certainly not the way someone who doesn't care acts, but had I
not seen her with this work I would never have known how seriously
she took her responsibility as a teacher. Many incidents like this have
taught me to give my colleagues the benefit of the doubt. They may be
disheartened and they may not be innovative or creative, but that doesn't
mean that they don't care about their profession or their students.

As I explained earlier, the structure of urban schools cuts off one constituency from another and creates divisions between groups. Few urban
schools give faculty common time to plan or discuss shared problems.
Young teachers aren't given access to the specialized knowledge older

teachers have, and older teachers can't tap the vitality and new ideas their young colleagues bring to the classroom. If new teachers could see portraits of many of their cynical, pessimistic, older colleagues when they began their careers, the newcomers would be astonished. Very often teachers who have been working for many years have watched the enthusiasm with which they began their career steadily eroded. When the school system gives them opportunities to replenish themselves, they often do. Unfortunately, urban schools are notorious for the poor quality of their professional development; more often than not, inservice workshops are useless, even insulting. Teachers see that their ideas are not valued or respected, and in response many stop struggling to make themselves heard. They have so often been ordered to use a new curriculum or method that they become skeptical about all change.

Many dedicated teachers respond to the demoralization and alienation within the faculty by focusing entirely on their own classrooms. They shut their classroom doors, literally and figuratively. While this strategy has the undeniable advantage of helping you ration your energy, the atomization of the faculty makes the school more dysfunctional because many problems can only be solved collectively.

How can you be active in staff life without becoming embattled and isolated? I almost always found that if I acknowledged the extreme hardship of our working lives and followed this with positive suggestions of steps we might take to improve a situation, my colleagues would listen. Like their students, they want to succeed but they feel overwhelmed by conditions that are beyond their control. Your colleagues need your vitality and idealism; you need their knowledge and perspective.

But even as you begin your first years of teaching, you need to think about your future. What will you do to resist the forces that have depleted these teachers? How will you sustain your energy and idealism? Conditions in urban schools will treat you no more kindly than they have your colleagues. You can easily become the teacher whose passivity and negativity make you shudder if you don't think through a personal program for professional growth. You cannot count on the school or your colleagues to nurture your development as a teacher, so join the organizations and professional associations that can keep you intellectually alert and well informed. In the years that I taught in the suburbs, I was involved in organizations of English and journalism teachers, and I noticed when I began to teach in the city schools how rarely information that I had taken for granted—for instance, national debates about curriculum—permeated the school walls. It's easy to become isolated in your school, cut off from professional discussions about developments in teaching and content, so you need to create your own connections to the educational community beyond the school walls by joining professional organizations, reading relevant publications, and attending conferences. New networks of urban teachers have developed over the last few years, most of them with an online presence. An hour or two of surfing the web will locate many resources that can help you with planning and problem solving or provide solace.

After you feel that you've become acclimated to your job, talk to teachers who still enjoy their work after many years, and ask them how they've done it. I'm certain they will have helpful suggestions for you. One marvelous social studies teacher I know throws out all her plans after each term so that she starts from scratch each semester; a friend who is a stupendous English teacher creates a new course every few years so that he can teach a current interest; a friend who was a math teacher returned to school for a degree in literature and became a teacher of English in her 15th year of teaching. The strategies are as different as the people, but urban teachers who still enjoy their work after 10 years have developed a plan to sustain their satisfaction.

Books, Materials, and Supplies

In most urban schools, materials are a serious problem, especially for new teachers who have not accumulated their personal stash of books, wall decorations, and supplies. Supplies are usually ordered 6 months before you need them, perhaps in April for the following September, and the amount of money allocated is quite paltry. As a result of the chronic underfunding of schools, supplies and teaching materials are scarce, and high-quality materials even scarcer. You should anticipate developing your own.

Most teachers pay for teaching supplies out of their own pockets because they need the materials to do an adequate job. In schools in poor neighborhoods, parents can't provide supplies like pencils, paper, and crayons, so teachers buy them for their classes because they're indispensable. Everyone draws the line at subsidizing the school system at a different spot, and I would never say that one person's limit is morally defensible and another's is not. Teachers face a dilemma: Society and government should fund urban schools adequately, but when kids can't learn because they don't have materials, teachers can't do their jobs well. On principle, I wouldn't buy chalk, though I did purchase pens, markers, and construction paper for journal covers. A friend of mine never bought supplies but provided clothes for needy students. You'll have to decide for yourself how much of your own time and money you're willing to spend because the school doesn't provide you and your students with what you require.

In many schools photocopying is very difficult to do, either because the machines are not accessible to teachers, or because paper is not available, or both. A school with 40 teachers may have only one machine, and you can bet on the fact that it will be broken on the morning you need to run off 25 copies for that day's work. Some urban schools still rely on the rexograph, or "ditto" machine, for classroom copies, so here again you'll have to decide for yourself whether paying for photocopies, if you can afford it, is a service you'll provide for the school system.

In many urban high schools and middle schools in poor neighborhoods, teachers are not permitted to issue books until the second or third week of classes. The rationale for this policy is that money for replacing books is scarce, and administrators anticipate that students who are likely to become truant will show up for the first days of the term but not return. If students receive books in these first days, the books will not be recovered, according to this rationale. (Of course, if teachers and students are denied texts and do nothing but busywork for the first several days, students will become demoralized, making the rationale for not distributing textbooks a self-fulfilling prophecy.) Be prepared for this predicament. Come to the opening of school with at least 1 or 2 weeks' worth of pre-prepared activities that are educationally worthwhile so that students see that your class will be valuable.

The quality of books that you'll find in the school will depend on the specific school and district in which you're teaching, but, in general, the poorer the community the school serves, the worse the resources, including books. Don't be surprised if the school has no books you want to use or not enough books for you to assign one to each student! Many schools give teachers a "classroom set" of textbooks that students can never take home to study or read. The book shortage means that you'll have to create your own materials. This might be a blessing because you won't be forced to use a boring, outdated textbook. On the other hand, you'll be working doubly hard to create these materials rather than simply supplementing a text.

Many urban schools now require teachers to use "scripted" materials in targeted subjects, like literacy and math. For some new teachers, those who are so overwhelmed with organizing the classroom that they don't have time or energy to develop their own lessons, these highly detailed plans are like manna from heaven. For others, the script is confining and oppressive. If you fall into the latter category, try to make the best of the situation by concentrating your creativity and inventiveness on the subjects in which you have more freedom. Very few teachers have to use scripted materials for all subjects and levels, so everyone should be prepared to develop at least some materials independently.

Space

Most of the time new teachers receive the worst rooms. Often they are given programs in which they have to travel to several classrooms, lugging their materials with them. The physical environment in most urban schools is a disgrace, and, in general, the poorer the neighborhood, the worse the maintenance of the school and the classrooms. The only advice I can give you about this is that you have to find alternatives yourself. Let your supervisor know the reasons that the space is creating problems (falling plaster? leaking ceiling? no shades or blinds?), but don't expect him or her to remedy the situation. Repairs can take an entire semester or even a year in urban schools—when they are done at all.

Canvass the school to see what space is available; there may be a room that's free part of the time you need it. Use the space you have creatively, and invest in used furniture if that helps. Here again you'll be personally subsidizing a public school system in the world's richest country, but if a used desk or file cabinet makes your life easier, maybe a handout to the public school system is cheaper than your anguish. If you want to make a change that may be permanent—like putting colored shelf-paper on windows, as several colleagues of mine did to keep the sun from beating down on students—you should mention this to your supervisor.

Clerical Work

Because of requirements in the new federal legislation I referred to earlier, all schools that accept federal aid must report far more data to the government, like test scores and teachers' qualifications. Almost all urban schools receive money earmarked for educating poor children,

which increases the amount of reporting. Because one unit of the bureaucracy doesn't communicate data to other offices, urban teachers
must complete an unbelievable amount of highly detailed clerical work,
often information they've already reported, though on a different form
for a different unit. The amount of clerical work also depends on the extent to which the state and district in which you teach regulate what you
teach and how you teach it. You may have to report attendance for the
day, week, month, and term. You may have to fill out grids that show
you are complying with curriculum standards that are linked to standardized test scores. You will have to complete forms without knowing
their purpose as well as forms whose purpose is self-evident. All of this
paperwork comes on top of assessing students' work, assigning grades,
and planning lessons.

You'll need a method for handling the paperwork. In my first few
years of teaching, I developed a system that helped me deal with student
papers and clerical work that kept it from being a sword of Damocles
that killed every weekend. The strategy worked well for me when I
began teaching in the city schools, though I had to devote more time to
paperwork than I ever had before. I always completed clerical work in
school, during my lunch hour or "prep" period, and stayed after school
a day or two a week to mark student papers and plan my lessons. I
know fine teachers who can't face staying at school, or cannot remain
too late because of family responsibilities or second jobs, so they take
clerical work home, to complete while they watch TV. Some people
find it works to devote one day of the weekend to planning and clerical
work. Other people come very early to school. During the first few years
on the job, experiment with different techniques to find one that allows
you to get your paperwork under control.

If schools were organized and funded appropriately, new teachers
would have adequate resources, the easiest teaching programs, and co-
herent professional support to help them adjust to their new careers. As
you can see from my description of the reality you'll encounter, exactly
the opposite holds in most urban schools. In the next chapter I explain
what you can expect from your supervisors and the teachers' union as
you begin your teaching career in a city school.

Your Relations with Teachers, the Union, and Administrators

5

In most urban schools, a kind of warfare exists between teachers and their supervisors. The battle can be a guerrilla operation in which both sides continually snipe or, less frequently, all-out war. In either case, relations are generally strained and hostile. Many new teachers are baffled and demoralized by these enervating battles, so it's important to understand why they occur.

Almost all the points I've made about the difference between teaching in urban and suburban school systems also apply to being an administrator in these settings. In city schools you have to work harder and have better teaching skills to achieve the same degree of success you'd have in an environment that didn't undercut your efforts. The same holds for administrators: Only those principals and assistant principals in city schools who are superb administrators can achieve satisfactory results; to really excel they have to be extraordinarily skillful and devote virtually all their waking hours to the job.

Administrators and Colleagues

As with teachers (and students), the bureaucracy sends school administrators many contradictory messages and provides them with almost no support. In most urban school districts, administrators at the school level have remarkably little power to make significant changes in the school's operations. Because decision making is top-down, administrators are put into an occupational double bind. Being an advocate for the school often means antagonizing higher-ups in the administration, who are responsible for promotions and other career rewards. The system's pressure on the supervisor to enforce foolish rules and policies places the conscientious supervisor in the same quandary as a teacher, but there's a vital distinction: Once teachers are tenured, they do not depend on the supervisor's good opinion of them for career advancement.

49

There's relatively little that a school-site administrator can do to help or harm the career of a competent tenured teacher; the system's procedures and regulations, including the union contract, limit prerogatives.

Rules and mandates promulgated in the bureaucracy continually threaten successful operations, whether it's an after-school program, a new course, or a new curriculum. One historian who's been involved with many school reform efforts described the bureaucracy's relationship to innovative programs this way: Anything different is continually picked at, like a scab, until all distinctive elements are eliminated.

Teachers, who are near the bottom of the hierarchy, depend on the school-site administrators to protect them and their programs. For instance, one year all high schools in New York were mandated to separate 9th-grade students into special units, or "houses," in an attempt to stem the dropout rate, which research showed was greatest in 9th grade. However, Humanities High School, where I was teaching, placed students of all grades in elective courses and had a negligible dropout rate. The system's mandate was obviously detrimental to the school's unique curriculum, yet we were subject to it. As the school's spokesperson, the principal had to negotiate with the bureaucracy to obtain a waiver. Her ability and willingness to make a case for the school's needs would determine whether it would continue to offer its widely admired elective program. As a newly appointed principal, she was in a precarious position; not by nature combative, she hesitated to engage in a battle to protect the school's unusual features. She was able to delay implementation of the initiative, but ultimately the bureaucracy prevailed and the school was forced to comply. Over the course of 5 years, many of the school's distinctive features were eroded in a similar pattern, until it became much like any other comprehensive high school.

To obtain their positions, principals must have friends or sponsors within the bureaucracy and be thought of as "team players." But to protect their schools, they must know how to exert pressure on the bureaucracy; and within their schools they must be perceived as fair and supportive leaders. Unfortunately, people who have this combination of talents, as well as knowledge about sound educational practice and a willingness to work 12 hour days, are rare.

Moreover, someone whose personality and strengths make him or her a fine leader at one school won't necessarily be the best principal of another school, yet urban school bureaucracies deal with school principals and administrators like they do with all people, as interchangeable commodities, so they're often plucked from one school, where they've been successful, and placed in another, where they're out of place. Few people naturally have the combination of gifts required to run a school, department, or program, and the school system does almost nothing to help administrators to develop them. As a result, many people who care about education and children and were respected teachers plunge in over their heads when they become administrators.

One of the department heads I worked under in the city schools illustrates the phenomenon I've just explained. Mr. X, who was chairperson of the English Department, was so disorganized and overwhelmed by paperwork that his office, which contained the phones, was entirely covered from the floor to mid-waist in old memos, exams, test papers, and compositions. The phones were buried in these papers, as was his desk, so that teachers would hear the phone ringing but couldn't answer it—because we couldn't find it! Just as important, no one could call the security desk or the dean's office in an emergency.

Mr. X was a sensitive, literate individual who had been a creative, well-regarded English teacher in another high school some years before, but he was not an effective department head for this school. In another setting Mr. X's disorganization would have been less detrimental because the demands made on him would have been more limited. However, Mr. X's weaknesses as an administrator were compounded exponentially by the extraordinary burdens placed on supervisors in this large comprehensive high school serving students with very poor skills. In addition to overseeing the state exams given in all New York high schools, Mr. X was required to monitor paperwork on countless other projects. Almost all our students qualified for compensatory education courses, a situation entailing substantial recordkeeping: pre-tests, post-tests, purchase orders, and budget reports. Almost all our students took the state competency test in writing two or three times before they passed it. The test was taken in triplicate, but only one copy was sent to the state; the results as well as the actual tests had to be stored in the school.

During my 5 years in the school, teachers in the English Department were involved in at least 10 different curriculum projects; each project, which the department head was obligated to supervise, generated several reports. As the supervisor of more than 20 teachers, Mr. X was obligated to write observations of each person at least once a year, as well as reports on dozens of ongoing specially funded grants and projects. Unfortunately, Mr. X's control of the paper flow was, to say the least, inadequate for the volume the English Department generated.

In addition, the school system defined his job as a "line" position, conveying and enforcing regulations, whereas the teachers' expectations were that he would represent their concerns and needs to the principal and the district. Had Mr. X been able to balance these contradictory demands, he would have had some credibility with the staff. However, his gentleness and timidity coupled with his disorganization made him an object of scorn among the people he had to supervise. Accomplishing the most straightforward task, like organizing and grading state exams, became Herculean because relations between Mr. X and department members were so unpleasant.

I've described this situation in considerable detail to demonstrate that the hostility between teachers and administrators needs to be understood in light of conditions in the school system, not just characteristics of individuals. I was no less frustrated than my colleagues with Mr. X's ineffectiveness, but understanding how the demands of the job magnified his weaknesses helped me to maintain a civil relationship.

Still, the strife between administrators and teachers makes life especially difficult for new teachers because if they identify themselves too closely with supervisors who are widely disliked, they isolate themselves from their colleagues. Conversely, if new teachers ally themselves with faculty members, they risk being alienated from their supervisors, who evaluate their performance. You need to keep in mind that your colleagues will not expect a new teacher, one who is not tenured, to become embroiled in conflicts between the administration and the staff. As an untenured teacher you have little legal protection, so you are very vulnerable; and your colleagues know this, even if they don't articulate it to you. They don't expect new teachers to risk their careers by confronting supervisors, and you shouldn't have that expectation either.

What if the situation is the opposite—you think the teachers are responsible for the poor relations between administrators and staff? In fact, this was my reaction at the first department meeting: I was stunned at the way people spoke to Mr. X! I had worked with him on a curriculum project the month before school opened and thought him intelligent and genial, so I was unnerved by the antipathy that greeted him. As the months went on, I saw the department's situation in a different light, and by Thanksgiving I fully appreciated my colleagues' anger.

I think that your point of view about who's culpable may change after you've spent some time as a teacher, so even if you feel quite certain that the faculty is causing problems, bite your lip until you're really settled into the school. Your colleagues will have a very long memory of your actions if you publicly side with a supervisor against them. In my experience, these conflicts are seldom so clear-cut that you want to risk your credibility with your colleagues to defend the actions of a supervisor, or vice versa, in your first year or two of teaching.

My advice to maintain cordial relations with colleagues is based on another reality of life in most urban schools. If your situation is typical, your contact with your supervisor will be perfunctory. He or she will probably be too busy to help you out with your classroom, and so you'll have to rely on colleagues for assistance. The school bureaucracy's greatest concern is the appearance of sound educational practice, not the reality, and this fact of life governs administrators' work. If you're using a brilliant teaching strategy, no one will see or ask, so your effort won't be acknowledged. Similarly, if no one sees that you're utterly confounded about how to teach a subject, your problem doesn't count as a serious one because it's hidden, so you'll receive neither blame nor assistance. However, if you knowingly or unknowingly violate a regulation and the violation is noticed, the issue will receive immediate attention. Because your adhesion to school rules and your students' scores on standardized tests will receive more attention from most school administrators than your teaching ability, you need to rely on your colleagues for help in your classroom.

What if the negativity of the teachers is so overwhelming, their overt statements of prejudice so frequent, that you find yourself totally isolated from your colleagues? If the principal or department head seems sympathetic, you may be tempted to develop a close relationship with the administrator as a way to set the other teachers straight. Trying to take on your colleagues alone, as a new teacher, is quite unwise, even if you seem to have an administrator's support. The comparison may seem grisly, but it's apt: Think of prisoners and the warden. The warden can't protect prisoners from the wrath of other inmates and, in fact, doesn't usually make more than a nominal effort because protection of a highly unpopular inmate who's viewed as being a favorite might disrupt the status quo to the point that rebellion would break out.

Some of the best teachers I've helped prepare, those who work in really tough urban schools and view urban teaching as a long-term commitment, tell me that they have found one piece of advice especially helpful: I have drilled into them that it's essential both to acquire an "insider's" knowledge of how the school functions and also maintain an "outsider's" critique. When people start their teaching jobs, they are usually excited (and anxious!) about what they will do that is different, fresh, and new. They bring a clear picture of what improved schools and teaching look like. These are the seeds of your outsider critique. You've identified a limitation in schools and teaching and want to see a change. However, it's normal to lose track of our original outsider views as we become socialized to a new environment and acquire an insider point of view. You need to work, consciously, to maintain this tension between your insider/outsider perspectives. That's an especially difficult task in urban schools because of their insularity. Even the language of school people marks them as insiders. Many times I have to ask teachers in my classes to translate the lingo used in New Jersey schools to describe students and policies because the abbreviations and terms I know are from New York and California.

One of the surest ways to maintain your outsider critique is to consistently touch base with your students. It may seem odd to consider them outsiders, given the time they spend in the school, but students are almost never asked what they think of policies and practices. Yet, as I discuss more fully in the next chapter, they can provide some of the most valuable information about what you—and the school—should do differently to help them all succeed.

I have never worked in a school in which my own political beliefs were shared by a majority of the teachers, but I was able to establish a respectful working relationship with my colleagues. However, I realize that my situation is not necessarily shared by minority teachers in schools with a predominantly White faculty, because minority teachers may experience more acute social isolation. The advice I have comes from an extreme situation, from my colleague at New Jersey City University who weathered isolation and intense, overt hostility from other teachers in her school during the acrimonious strikes over community control of schooling in New York in 1968–1969. These strikes bitterly divided teachers and heightened racial tensions in the city for many years to come. My colleague was a new, inexperienced teacher who very much wanted help in applying ideas she had learned in her preparation to teach. Her colleagues cut her off entirely, but she developed her connections with community activists and parents, drawing on them for sustenance and assistance. She established a cordial working relationship with one other teacher, with whom she ate lunch and discussed teaching. Perhaps because of her close relations with parents and community activists, my colleague weathered the hostility and had a gratifying career as a city teacher. I think we can generalize that the larger the school, the more likely you are to find at least a few empathetic and helpful colleagues, but if you are really scorned by your colleagues, you'll need to find support outside of the school, in professional networks and community groups.

The relationships you'll want to have with your colleagues and supervisors will probably reflect your sense of whether you consider urban teaching your career or whether you'll be moving on to another job in not too long. The more confident you are that urban teaching is a long-time commitment, the more attention you'll want to pay to establishing yourself as an insider. This, in turn, makes the importance of retaining your outsider critique all the more important. People who view teaching as a temporary job, as is often the case of young college graduates who enter through the alternate-route programs that require little advance preparation, face another problem in their relations with colleagues. Career teachers who have gone through traditional teacher education sometimes resent newcomers who have taken what to them is the shortcut of the alternate route. They observe that alternate-route teachers often have not mastered skills, especially relating to classroom management, that are usually learned during student teaching. More than a few experienced teachers bristle at the presumption that teaching is not a profession that requires considerable preparation and skill to do well.

Their resentment may also be compounded by an issue that is rarely articulated. Teachers in urban schools who have gone through traditional teacher education are often the first in their families to attend college; most come from lower-middle-class and working-class backgrounds; many have worked their way through school, often living at home. On the other hand, many teachers entering through alternate-route programs, especially those targeting recruits from elite colleges, have parents with considerable formal education and enough income to pay college tuition and room and board. Though as a society we do not like to acknowledge that social class exists, let alone that it influences our life prospects, class tensions do arise among teachers. Another factor that creates social conflicts for many alternate-route teachers, especially young people who have never before worked in full-time jobs: They may be more likely than first-year teachers who graduated from traditional programs (and became socialized to the "insider" viewpoint during their student teaching experience) to convey a critique of the school—and its teachers.

As someone who was a career teacher and went through a traditional program of teacher education, I can understand the resentment teachers prepared in traditional programs may feel toward young alternate-route teachers. On the other hand, I had many of the characteristics of alternate-route candidates recruited to teaching. Like them, teaching was my first full-time job. I took up teaching without thinking that it would be my career, and although I had to support myself when I decided to take courses toward my certification, I had been a full-time undergraduate at U.C. Berkeley, supported by my parents. I value what I brought to teaching as an idealistic, young teacher, but I also see what I needed to learn from my colleagues. My advice to alternate-route recruits sensing unfriendliness from colleagues is to face that there's likely more going on here than is being openly discussed. Try to look beyond your colleagues' hostility to see what they can teach you. Your contribution to the school and kids will be greater if you do.

The Teachers' Union

In most urban school districts, except those in southern states that prohibit the practice, when you become a teacher you automatically have the equivalent of union dues deducted from your salary. Union membership is optional, but your paycheck will have deducted from it that portion of union dues that the union demonstrates has been spent for collective bargaining expenses. The rationale for the laws that permit this practice, called deduction of an "agency fee," is that all teachers benefit from the contract the union negotiates and the services it provides, like filing grievances for teachers who think their rights under the contract have been violated. Having classes held to a certain maximum is generally a contractual issue; negotiations for your salary and benefits, like health care, is another.

I've written elsewhere on the subject of teacher unionism and don't have space here to explore it fully, but I do want to put in a plug for what the teachers' unions should be, as opposed to the form teacher unionism takes in most big-city school systems. I think if you understand the purpose and potential of the union, you may look at the union differently.

Schools are workplaces, and as in most workplaces that are divided between managers and workers, the two groups see issues differently. In wealthy suburban school districts teachers are treated with considerably more dignity and respect than they are in city schools. They consider themselves professionals and are in the main treated that way by the school system. For instance, the school year opened in Bedford Hills, a wealthy suburb of New York where I taught after moving from California, with a catered reception for new faculty. We met the district administrators, who had read our résumés and were acquainted with our backgrounds, and we discussed educational issues.

My initiation as an employee of the New York City schools began at the central administration building in Brooklyn, where I was assigned an identification number and fingerprinted. There was absolutely no pretense that I was a professional or that there was anything special or valuable about me as a teacher. Like secretaries and cooks, teachers punched in and out of school on a time clock. The practice continued until the union negotiated alternate procedures for recording teachers' work schedules. Teachers in urban schools are treated like other city workers, and they have no illusions that the system appreciates them or considers them special by virtue of their education, skills, or talents.

One of the primary reasons that teacher unionism was born and reborn in city schools is that city teachers simply can't think of themselves only as professionals because of the way they're treated. Every minute and action is subject to regulation. If you come late to school, your salary is docked, though it's not increased if you stay late voluntarily every day to tutor students. You're subjected to one indignity after another, like being told to fill out forms three different ways because one office won't send a copy of the form to another. You're subjected to a barrage of insulting and nonsensical directives that show the lack of knowledge highly placed school officials have of real conditions in schools.

Many teachers view the union as irrelevant to their teaching and pay little attention to its affairs. Some see the union as a barrier to school improvement. Although I understand why they feel this way, their response saddens me because I know from my experience that the teachers' union can defend teachers' economic interests and, at the same time, be a force for progressive change in schools. When I began my teaching career in Hayward, California, I helped build our local teachers' union, which recruited many of the district's teachers who were most interested in curriculum reform and defending students' well-being. We were active in the union because it was a vehicle for us to influence policies that affected us professionally. We monitored how the district spent its funds and publicized expenditures we considered wasteful; we demanded—and won—staff participation in planning professional development activities; we organized parents to help us hold down class size; and we struggled for well-deserved salary increases. The teachers' union had excellent relations with minority parents because of our active support of community and labor struggles.

For most city teachers—and parents, too—it's hard to imagine that teachers' unions can be dynamic, democratic, and progressive. But they can be! The union should be your voice, exposing the system's problems and organizing parents and citizens to join with teachers to improve conditions. Unfortunately, urban teacher unions have become bureaucratic themselves, and in the largest cities, the union leadership is removed from the concerns of the teachers. "The union" has become something separate from its members, so that school people, teachers and administrators alike, say, "The union doesn't permit that," although the union contract is approved (or rejected) by a vote of the union membership and negotiated by officers who are elected and paid by union members.

In many urban schools the union has little presence, and hardly anyone wants to be elected "building rep," or union representative, because it's a great deal of work that offers minimal rewards, usually a small amount of time out of the classroom and perhaps a token financial reimbursement. The building rep funnels information from the union leadership to members and meets with the principal about issues of concern to the faculty. However, in schools that have weak union organization, the union's presence comes to bear mostly at the district level and in the contract the union leadership negotiates. For these reasons, unless you make a special effort to become involved in the union, it will be a shadowy presence in your professional life.

Even if you can't see yourself becoming active in the union to improve it, you should attend the union meetings held in your school and become acquainted with the building rep. Both are important sources of information for you. I hate to say this, but I must: In many urban schools the building rep is not a person who is considered an exceptional teacher, though he or she is almost never someone who is incompetent. There's often a division between teachers who take care of union affairs and those who are deeply immersed in their teaching, although in my experience the most effective building reps are those who are respected as teachers. Still, many times your building rep can help you when you run into barriers in trying to do a better job of teaching. The advice my building rep gave me about how to handle the coats-in-class rule illustrates the kind of guidance he or she can provide. Even building reps who are not themselves stellar instructors can give you information that will help you to become one, by learning how to circumvent regulations without defying supervisors and imperiling your position.

Some new teachers who have not had experience with unions may be afraid that they will be scrutinized by administrators if they go to union meetings or have contact with the building rep. This is almost never the case in urban schools, where the union's presence is accepted without question. Can you trust that concerns you express to the building rep will be kept in confidence, as they should be? A building rep would almost never reveal confidential information because his or her credibility with the teachers would be lost, and with it the ability to influence relations between the staff and administration. Especially in schools with terrible working conditions and a totally demoralized staff, you may find a building rep who is more interested in currying favor with administrators than helping colleagues, and then you're stuck. If you remain in the school until you're tenured, your only choice is to work with like-minded colleagues to take over the union by voting in a new building rep, perhaps yourself.

It can be hard to see the potential for teachers' unions in urban school systems because often the unions are so stale, so fixed on maintaining the status quo. But all kinds of unions throughout the country, in fact all over the world, are in crisis right now, and teachers' unions are no exception. They can't figure out how to respond to the drastically changed political and economic landscape and the demands being made on education. The generation of teachers entering urban schools now will have to provide a new direction for teacher unionism if teachers are going to alter conditions in their schools. And nowhere is this more important than in urban school districts, where teachers are the most stable, powerful constituency for maintaining education as a publicly funded, democratically controlled service.

Unlike the administrators of the school system, your union officers are directly elected, by you and other teachers. A few urban school systems have seen entrenched union leaders defeated by reform caucuses, who have restored public confidence in the teaching staff by advocating progressive change in schooling and in politics. If teachers become involved in the union to make it fight for their ideals, teacher unionism will become a powerful partner in the social movement that's needed to improve urban schools. The unions have enormous potential, but classroom teachers have to transform them from the dues-collecting machines they've too often become. I hope you'll be part of that effort. Your voice in education, your working conditions, and salary are at stake—as are your students' futures.

6

Your Students

The question of whether children in urban classrooms are different from kids elsewhere has been a source of contention in educational research and policy for more than a century. It's an important issue because the starting point for our decisions about how we teach should be analysis of our students. Although I think that we can't fully understand how teachers and students behave in schools without taking into account school structures and policies, in addition we all bring differing knowledge, abilities, and beliefs that affect how we function in the classroom.

Examining my own experience, I realize that my students in the city schools were different from those I had worked with in the suburbs. In Chapters 1 and 2, I explained that "urban" shouldn't be considered an either/or condition. I think the same holds true of students who've been raised in cities; they differ from their counterparts in the suburbs in ways that have to do with the distinctive aspects of city life. When I taught in Malverne and Bedford Hills, two small suburbs of New York City, I noticed that teenagers who had only recently moved to these suburbs were more sophisticated and had an edge, an energy that their suburban classmates lacked. In Bedford Hills, the city kids were White, the children of well-educated professionals who had lived in Manhattan's prosperous sections. In Malverne, the students were usually sons and daughters of African American civil servants who had lived in working-class communities in Brooklyn and Queens. In both situations, the suburban students and I saw differences that were clearly a result of students having lived in city neighborhoods.

Teachers and students bring attitudes and behaviors to school that they've acquired in living in particular places, and cities are no different from other locales in making their mark on the way we view life and respond to it, in ways that are both potentially positive and negative in a school setting. Kids who are raised in neighborhoods where the harshness of life is immediately apparent, as it is in poor communities, are often used to defending themselves verbally and physically. If their families have had negative experiences with intrusive governmental agencies, they may be very concerned about their privacy and withhold information you request in order to help them. If they are used to hearing people speak their minds bluntly, they will expect to respond this way to you and their classmates.

I've heard people describe city kids as being "street smart," in contrast to being "school smart." I really dislike that characterization because it implies that the astuteness and maturity that children have developed by living in a demanding environment aren't applicable to the learning that should occur in school. I'd argue that when teachers are knowledgeable and respectful about the ways city life can support their efforts to teach, "street smart" is simply "smart."

Applying Information About Cultural Differences

Even if urban kids are different from those in the suburbs or rural communities, students' characteristics can't be understood in isolation from the conditions in urban schools. For this reason one thread of research on urban schools—scholarship identifying important variations in the ways different groups accommodate to the rigid, impersonal character of urban schools—is especially helpful to teachers when it is used wisely. However, this research has to be used as background information, not as a formula that predicts the behavior and performance of students. Moreover, it shouldn't be used, as it sometimes is, to blame children and parents for academic failure, thereby justifying the educational system's historic and contemporary failure to provide all children with a high-quality education. Applying knowledge about cultural differences to teaching is perplexing because we are simultaneously members of many different categories and groups. People may share a nationality but hold to different religions, be considered members of the same racial category but come from different class backgrounds, share the same language but differ in gender and sexual orientation. Many teachers are wary of using information about cultural differences because they see how easily it leads to stereotyping, to robbing people of their individuality. However, the commonly espoused belief that "I don't see color (or class, or ethnicity, or gender) because kids are kids" ignores key political, economic, and social influences on school success.

Much has been written about the role of culture in school achievement, and you should be knowledgeable about this scholarship. More often than not, the media present a superficial, sensationalized version of scholarly debates about the effects of culture on academic success, so if your acquaintance with this topic is based primarily on conversations with friends, your own impressions, and the popular media, you need to educate yourself by reading in more depth or taking an intellectually serious course. Not all college courses that have "multicultural education" in the title will give you the background you need to think through the topic. In fact, one researcher found that workshops given to new teachers in Los Angeles didn't change their teaching practice at all and, for some, actually increased the tendency to think about students stereotypically. I think an ideal course acquaints you with key scholarship and helps you identify and reflect on cultural assumptions, especially those that are tacit, ones that we take for granted. Hopefully the course will help you apply the insights to your teaching.

I should clarify what I mean when I use the word *culture* because the word has two definitions—"culture" in the anthropological sense and also as a synonym for *civilization* or *erudition*. Culture to anthropologists is the meaning a group of people assign to events and objects in their lives; in this definition, culture is not limited to people who are well educated. Everyone who talks and socializes with other people has a culture.

One idea that my students have found helpful in making sense of cultural differences is to understand that many of the notions and categories that we take for granted are created by the society or, put another way, are "socially constructed." At a particular time and place, societies assign variations among people different meanings. For instance, many groups that we call "nationalities" today, like Italians, were called "races" at the turn of the 19th century. In this country we identify skin color as a determinant of race, generally seeing race as a "Black/White" dichotomy, but this is definitely not a universal way of making sense of racial difference. We can identify biological differences between males and females, but the social implications of these differences have changed a great deal since I began my teaching career. In 1973, at the interview for my first teaching job, the soft-spoken 60-something superintendent asked me in a kindly tone, "Why is it that such an attractive young lady isn't married?" Today his question is illegal to ask of a job applicant.

Because we are immersed in our own culture, we take it for granted and often forget that we bring to all our social interactions a particular cultural frame of reference that has not been shared by all people at all times. If you've traveled to foreign countries or spots in the United States that differ significantly from your home territory, you've probably been struck by cultural variations. When I have the opportunity, I enjoy browsing through guidebooks written in other languages for foreign visitors to New York City because they present so many aspects of city life differently from the way I'm used to viewing it. One guidebook written for French travelers on a budget warns its readers that in U.S. restaurants you'll be considered rude if you ask for "the toilet." Due to our Puritan background, we say "bathroom" or "restroom," the book cautions, rather than the straightforward "w.c." (water closet) or "toilette" used in France. The book pokes fun at our laws prohibiting drinking beer and wine in public areas, like parks or street benches, because the French treat wine like we do soft drinks.

Using knowledge about cultural differences while avoiding stereotypes requires that teachers regard information about cultural differences in the same way that competent doctors use epidemiological data. They keep it in the back of their mind to inform their decisions, but they don't automatically make it the diagnosis. A chest pain in a man who's a member of group that's at high risk for heart disease might be caused by indigestion from a chili dog, or it might indicate a heart attack. We'd expect the doctor to question and examine the patient as part of the process of making a diagnosis, using information from clinical observation along with his or her knowledge of the risk factors for heart disease among different groups.

The same process occurs in classrooms. Your knowledge of cultural factors is by itself an inadequate basis for making instructional decisions, yet data about cultural differences will often be useful. Because conditions in urban school systems pressure you to treat your students as an undifferentiated mass, you'll find that the more information you have about your students' backgrounds, the better equipped you are to deal with them as individuals. Knowing that your student Khalifa is Muslim, that observant Muslims don't eat from sunup to sundown during Ramadan, and that Ramadan falls at a certain time of year doesn't necessarily explain why Khalifa is sleeping in class, but it suggests explanations that you'll want to consider.

The more information you can tap into about students' lives outside school, the more efficient you'll become in developing hypotheses and solutions in your teaching. How can you acquire this data? The starting point should be an acknowledgment that your own experiences, expectations, and values are not necessarily generalizable to your students. You'll miss important cues that you should pursue when students express their ideas if you aren't alert to the information you're receiving.

In this regard, you need to consider yourself an anthropologist, putting aside many of your ideas about how people should and do act, seeking alternative explanations for your students' behavior and thinking. In suggesting that you think as an anthropologist, I need to clarify that you seek this information in order to learn from your students, not to study them as research subjects.

Recall that one of the characteristics of urban school systems is that they serve a highly diverse group of students. Especially if you are like most new, young teachers who have attended school in small towns or suburbs with other people who are like you, learning to work with students and parents who are culturally different from yourself is a significant challenge. I use the term "culturally different" because in urban schools especially, teachers face students who are culturally different from themselves, though the extent of difference varies. For example, if you are a White, middle-class teacher who is an English monolingual working with recent Chinese immigrants from poor and working-class families, the gulf in life experience between you and your students will probably be quite substantial and made more so by language differences. If you are a mature, upper-middle-class female African American who has changed careers and you teach poor and working-class African American and Chicano students, your students also will be culturally different from you, but the dissimilarities you experience may be a by-product of the way "race" is configured by class, gender, and generational differences. Teachers raised and educated in the same neighborhood as their students often have an overlapping cultural frame, but even here their experiences of the community may differ in significant ways. Though raised in the same neighborhood, they may have seen it differently because of their family's structure, values, and economic position.

If you use scholarship about culture as background information wisely, it can help you make sense of how these cultural differences may influence school achievement. One theory you may find illuminating is anthropologist John Ogbu's categorization of minorities into two groups, "voluntary" and "involuntary" minorities. Ogbu distinguished between students who are voluntary minorities, who have emigrated to this country voluntarily for political or economic reasons, and those belonging to involuntary minorities, whose presence is due to their subjugation as a colonized people or as slaves. Although both kinds of minorities face discrimination, especially if they are dark-skinned or speak another language, they respond differently because of their disparate cultural frames of reference. Voluntary minorities often view racial discrimination and poverty as obstacles to be bypassed; their frame of reference is the society they left behind. They may view themselves as fortunate to have free public education and may have come to this country specifically for our schools. On the other hand, for involuntary minorities, current instances of oppression are often experienced as examples of their permanently subordinate status, reminders that they may never be allowed to be equal. Because they have endured a history in which public schools have neglected and rejected them, a history that continues despite the fact that they are legally entitled to an equal education, involuntary minorities have good reason to be suspicious of school people.

Researchers have refined Ogbu's work and criticized many of his contentions. Because of this new scholarship, we have an understanding of the complex relationships between culture and school achievement, yet key questions remain unanswered. For instance, we know that the age at which kids emigrate is important in their acculturation and their attitude toward schooling, as are parental attitudes about whether they will return to their native land. Historians have pointed to the respect and desire for education in the African American community that contradicts Ogbu's assumptions of how involuntary minorities regard education. This body of work suggests that responsibility for school failure lies much more with schools than with African Americans' attitudes, their cultural framework of reference. Other researchers have shown that pressing children to assimilate rapidly without helping them to retain community links can actually deter school success because it isolates children from peer support and undercuts parental authority.

Even if you teach in a school that seems to be homogeneous—for instance, a racially isolated school serving African American or Spanish-speaking immigrants—you will find that these categories obscure equally meaningful cultural variations. At King High School, I initially taught African American students who were born-and-bred New Yorkers, as well as students recently arrived in Harlem from small towns in the rural South. After I had taught for 2 years at King, the city altered its policy on admission to neighborhood high schools, and students from Jamaica and the U.S. Virgin Islands enrolled because King was safer than their neighborhood schools in Brooklyn. As a group they differed in their attitudes about school and teachers as much from the native New Yorkers as they did from one another. Similarly, Dominican, Puerto Rican, and Colombian students leaving the bilingual program all spoke Spanish but brought to the mainstream classes very different educational backgrounds and cultural frameworks.

When we analyze research about culture and learning in my graduate classes, some teachers tell me that Ogbu's categories help to explain differences they see in attitudes toward school and achievement. But I also hear from teachers who reject the voluntary/involuntary categorization as simplistic, and even insulting, and their criticism is echoed in research. I have included the concept because it focuses attention on the fact that that we all view school through a filter that has been produced by a complex interaction of forces, forces that we may not recognize but others may. The notion that people have different filters through which they see school life explains why teachers may find that some students are hostile to them from the start. The very presence of a European American, middle-class teacher may be suspect in the eyes of some students, especially in schools that have few faculty or administrators who share their cultural background. A teacher's higher social and economic status, as well as position in a school system that for most of its existence legally and openly discriminated against racial minorities, can make teachers appear to be supporters of the status quo, even if they are not. I think that in order to persuade your students and their parents that they will benefit from what you and the school can offer, you must understand their perspective. You need not share their viewpoint, but you need to acknowledge its existence. Generally speaking, you can win their confidence by making intellectual and social space in your classroom for cultural differences, acknowledging that all students bring life experiences, beliefs, and ideas that are no less worthy of examination than your own or those of classmates.

There is a *very* slippery slope between recognizing the influence of a cultural framework and allowing it to be an excuse for not teaching all kids well. For instance, Frank, a new high school biology teacher in a school with a large African American student population, wrote in one assignment for my class that he lauded Ogbu's work because it supported the observation that he and his colleagues had made in their lunchtime discussions: The problems of Black students were of their own making; they just didn't take advantage of all the opportunities the school afforded them. No, no, no! This conclusion is factually incorrect because it ignores the enormous amount of data that we have about the continuing presence of racism in schools and society. It is also a pedagogical cul-de-sac. When we blame students' lack of success in our classroom on the kids themselves or their parents, we remove the responsibility from ourselves for helping them to learn. Responses like Frank's highlight that teachers need more than data about cultural differences; they also must have a willingness to critique their own cultural frame of reference, an ability to be open, which is one of the attributes of reflective teaching.

Rosanna, a young, European-American second-year teacher who taught in a city grammar school serving many poor African American families, echoed Frank's anger at African American families. She expressed outrage that one of the 3rd graders in her class insisted that Blacks "can't trust White people." Rosanna argued that the remark was evidence of parents creating racial hostility that undercut her authority. However, a classmate disagreed with Rosanna's analysis, calling attention to news accounts of racism, like a brawl that started when two young children were called "dirty little niggers" by a city bus driver. Throughout the course Rosanna held to her belief that many of the African American parents fomented racial discord by discussing racial differences with their children. Rosanna argued that by placing the academic performance of involuntary minorities in a historical, social, and political context, we "excused" the behavior and attitude of students who were not taking advantage of what the public school system had to offer.

In my view, although Rosanna was intelligent, dedicated, and hard-working, like Frank she was on the road to becoming one of the alienated teachers she disliked. Because she was not open to viewing her school and herself as some students and parents did, she couldn't see that her students' life experiences might give them a perspective on race and schooling that, however upsetting to her, needed to be acknowledged. Despite her professed affection for her students, Rosanna probably communicated her anger to those students who did not share her beliefs about race. Inadvertently, she probably buttressed the mistrust the parents of some of her African American students had for her, European American teachers, and the school.

In contrast, another novice teacher in my class, Claudine—like Rosanna a young, European-American Staten Island resident—described to me how acquiring the ability to identify her own cultural frame of reference had totally altered the way she viewed her relations with students and parents, as well as her teaching. Although she had not begun her teaching career with this attitude, Claudine now considered cultural differences in the classroom an asset because they presented her with opportunities to learn about herself, her teaching, and life. In one of her assignments toward the end of the semester, Claudine recalled an incident that occurred when she had just begun teaching, in a Head Start program serving poor, African American children. "I was very confident, nurturing, energetic, and professional at 20 years of age," she noted, and the director and parents frequently complimented her on her teaching ability. Claudine had worked with a teacher's assistant and described the incident she had recently reconsidered:

> She was a Creole woman from the South, about 50 years of age, who was very lively and nurturing to the children. We worked well as a team. However, one day everything changed. I led the children out to the lunchroom where she had prepared their morning snack, sliced peaches in heavy syrup with a cup of milk. This was not my planned snack. "Milk would be too heavy with peaches in syrup. It will make their tummies sick," I said to her.
> "No, it will not," she answered. I became short with her. "I wrote juice for the menu. My mother always served me water or juice with this canned fruit. I feel safer serving juice to the children." At this point, she stated, "Well, where I'm from in Tennessee, my mamma served us peaches and cream. We never got sick. You see, I was raised on it. You're narrow in your cultural experience. You need to see other ways of life." I was humiliated and disgusted with this woman.

The conflict between Claudine and her assistant escalated, as the woman introduced "dolls, dances, and songs from her childhood." Consequently the assistant was removed from the room, and Claudine and she "rarely spoke again."

After describing the incident, Claudine analyzed how her opinion about it had changed. The important issue was not peaches and milk: The woman might have been right about the snack, or she might have been wrong. What was most critical was that Claudine had been unable to see that the aide, notwithstanding her lack of formal education, could provide her with information and insights that would help Claudine be a better teacher. She noted that a tremendous weight was lifted from her shoulders when she realized that she didn't have to know everything and could learn from her students and their parents. Claudine's new stance changed her self-conception as a teacher. Instead of being the expert, she was now a self-confident explorer, poised to pursue new interpretations of the curriculum—and life.

Judy, a new teacher in Brooklyn, explained how pivotal the teacher's attitude toward cultural differences is, contrasting her own performance in two schools. She had been teaching in a predominantly European

American, middle-class elementary school in Brooklyn, where the majority of students were third- and fourth-generation Italian Americans, like herself. Parents were active in their children's schooling, and students were competitive and highly motivated. Then the student population began to change, with Chinese, Russian, and Pakistani students attending. Judy explained:

> I found myself becoming impatient with this change. Academically, these children were not performing like the majority population of the school. The teachers, including myself, were having difficulty meeting and understanding their needs. I was guilty of taking on the attitudes of my peers, instead of developing my own. Teaching was getting harder and we didn't have the necessary resources to make it any easier.

Then she was transferred to another school, 30 blocks away, where students from what was called Yugoslavia, China, Puerto Rico, India, and Russia were the majority in the school. She realized that "my students were the resources all along. They come equipped with all the tools," but teachers have to know how to use them. Proudly, Judy wrote:

> For the past 5 months, my students have taught me how to educate them. They come to me with their own cultural experiences. We, as a class, laugh, discuss, and at times share so many emotions, such as tears, as we share our personal experiences.

Judy now brings students' parents and family members into the classroom to share their experiences and invited her own father to speak about his work on the Apollo space program. Teaching in this new way has completely altered her orientation as a teacher. "I stand before them changed," she observed.

Judy's quote that students bring the "tools" they need to succeed might make the task of acquiring proficiency in a new language seem automatic, as if students can easily learn English on their own. Au contraire! Anyone who's tried to become literate in a second language knows how arduous it is! The notion that we can plop students into English-speaking classes and expect them to master English—the sink-or-swim philosophy—is simply wrong for many kinds of children. I can't explore issues in second-language learning in this book with the seriousness they deserve because there's not room, but you should know that teachers certainly need to acquire knowledge about the process of second-language learning so that they can assist their students. They need to know, for example, how to tap the strength of the student's oral base in his or her native language and how to use small groups correctly to have students pratice oral language with their peers, to maximize communicative possibilities in the classroom. When Judy wrote that she saw that her students had the "tools" they needed to learn, I think she recognized that they bring skills and knowledge, cognitive and affective abilities, that teachers should use. One of those abilities is their linguistic strength in their native language. There are many, many others.

The Teacher as Learner

I think that the most successful urban teachers regard their students as people from whom they have much to learn as well as much to teach. They and their students regard the classroom as a community or family in which everyone's talents and abilities are respected. Though this stance toward teaching is valuable in classrooms everywhere, it is most difficult to sustain and most essential in urban schools because of the impersonal, anonymous environment.

In most urban schools teachers have little or no input about who is placed in their classes; the curriculum is mandated and sometimes instruction is controlled by "scripted" lesson plans that direct what you say and when to say it. Even if the teacher's compliance is not monitored directly, students' performance on standardized tests is used as a measure of the teacher's effectiveness. Materials and textbooks are often purchased by administrators at a central office without teacher or parent input; more often than not teachers find these books inappropriate for students in their classes and have not received adequate support in making a transition to new materials. For example, in elementary schools in an urban district in New Jersey that had been taken over by the state, each teacher had to use expensive new texts from a math series that the district's teacher advisory committee had recommended against purchasing.

The incessant pressure to cover predetermined material with students whose abilities and interests vary immensely encourages authoritarian teaching behaviors and custodial treatment of students. To resist these constraints, I think urban teachers need, first and foremost, the expectation that they are capable of helping their students to succeed academically and will do so. I know that in schools and maybe even education courses the role of expectations is expressed differently; what's emphasized is that the teacher must have high expectations for all students. But recent research on teachers' self-efficacy, individually and as a group in the school, confirms what my own student teachers concluded before this research was published: What's critical is that teachers be confident of their ability to teach and communicate their confidence and determination to teach all students.

In addition to this attitude, city teachers need to be especially skillful in three aspects of curriculum and instruction (the terms we use in education to describe what you teach and the way you teach it). Many wonderful books have been written to help new teachers, so I'll only sketch what I consider three essentials for city teachers. First, urban teachers should be knowledgeable about a broad range of teaching strategies because they teach children with such a vast assortment of needs. The more strategies you can call on, the more options you and your students will have to help them master material that you are obligated to teach. One key strategy you should master is the use of small groups, or cooperative learning, as it's often called. Second, you need to understand the content you teach well enough to ferret out the essence, so that you can help students master content that seems arcane, irrelevant, and remote—and often is. The most common complaint one hears from kids is that they don't see the reason they have to learn the material. The richer your background in the content knowledge you're teaching, the better able you'll be to figure out what to expand, cut out, and reshape to make the material motivating. Third, you need to create a sense of community in your classroom. You need to teach students the social skills that support academic learning and teach and reinforce the social norms that make the classroom a respectful environment, as I discuss in the next chapter. I think that really fine teachers everywhere are at least competent in all these areas, and for urban teachers to be even moderately effective with all of their students, they must be skilled in all three realms.

I don't think that successful urban teachers are necessarily extraordinary in all three areas, and they don't have to be because a strength in one domain can compensate for relative weakness in another. Like students, teachers bring different talents, and the key is to draw on your strengths while working to improve areas in which you are weak. I've seen teachers who are less knowledgeable than others about content, who prepare lessons that aren't intrinsically motivating to students; but these teachers do such a fine job of creating community spirit and trust that their students do what's expected of them, even if they aren't especially interested in the material. Sometimes teachers can draw on students' expectations that if teachers come from the neighborhood and are of the same race or culture, they'll be more understanding and committed. You still have to be able find ways to make the curriculum accessible, but you have an important asset that a teacher who's perceived differently doesn't. On the other hand, when I taught at Julia Richman and Martin Luther King Jr. High Schools, I worked with many African American students who viewed me suspiciously, expecting that I couldn't and wouldn't try to understand them or appreciate them. I think that my ability to create lessons that showed my students the power of their own ideas, lessons that connected instruction to their life experiences and validated it, helped me overcome the students' initial expectations about me as an older White teacher.

Much school reform rhetoric about helping all children master high standards stresses that the teacher should be the leader in a "community of learners." In this model, teachers learn from and with their students while maintaining responsibility for the orderly functioning of the classroom. Sadly, the notion that schools and classrooms should be "communities of learners" is generally enacted so poorly in urban schools that the concept itself is discredited. The kind of teaching called for in the model is immensely difficult but essential in urban schools because it establishes a dynamic between you and your students that is exactly the opposite of the relationship that the school system's bureaucratic practices pressure you to adopt. When you set up your classroom so that students respect and learn from one another, and you learn from them, you contradict the hierarchical nature of the school system. When you use teaching strategies that call for your students to interpret and analyze material so that you and they can critically compare ideas, you counter the "skill–drill–kill" sort of instruction that lends itself to the test-driven curricula that dominate in many urban school systems.

Including All Students

Both the difficulty and necessity of creating classrooms that are communities of learners have become more acute in the years since I left high school teaching in 1990; today urban teachers work in classrooms containing students with an even greater span of abilities and aspirations. Because of greatly increased immigration, classrooms contain significant numbers of students who need to master English. Often children who know little or no English receive instruction in ESL, or English as a Second Language, in pull-out programs. For 45 minutes the student is tutored, usually with other children, but for the rest of the school day this student is in the regular classroom. The "regular" teacher is responsible for helping the students learn English and keep up with content.

The other change that has accelerated since I left teaching in the city schools is a policy of integrating children in special education programs into regular classrooms. "Inclusion" or "integration" programs vary enormously from one school to another, but they all aim to put students with disabilities who previously were taught only in special education classes into regular classrooms. In inclusion classes, two teachers, one from special education, the other a "regular" classroom teacher, work together in a single classroom. Although we know from research that when inclusion is done well everyone benefits, frankly, it is most often not done the way it should be, especially in urban schools. For instance, especially in the beginning of their collaboration, the two teachers need to be given time and support to learn how to work together, but urban schools seldom have the resources to provide either time or quality support. Most often, teachers are assigned an inclusion class and have no choice and no special assistance. As one well-respected teacher told me, "When we receive our program, we all hold our breath that we haven't gotten the inclusion class."

These changes have resulted in classrooms that contain more of the students who were previously handed over to specialists to educate. The range of student abilities makes it all the more important for urban teachers to be masterful in the three areas I mentioned previously, but I want to stress one technique that has helped me in all three realms—cooperative learning.

I think that learning to use small groups well is a key skill for urban teachers for a number of reasons. Small-group work *when it is done correctly* makes students more responsible for their own learning; it empowers them within your classroom. Helping students to regulate their behavior and analyze their own learning is a considerable challenge in urban schools because the school structure and practices encourage teachers to be the boss and to treat their students in a custodial fashion; the structure and practices also encourage students to be passive. Kids' normal desire to interact, which is stymied in whole-class instruction, is tapped when they work in small groups. When students interact in a well-structured small-group activity that requires language, they teach one another language as well as content knowledge. I stress that small-group work needs to be carefully planned and carried out because if it is not done well, it can reinforce status inequalities among children. Please don't think using small groups is simply a matter of having the students push their seats together and do a worksheet! Learning to use small groups is a complex skill that has to be studied and practiced to be mastered.

Many city kids have adult responsibilities outside school, but in the classroom they are infantilized, denied control or power over what they do. This struck me one day as I watched my young daughter in a Manhattan park and observed a 9-year-old boy playing with his friends and minding his 2-year-old brother for several hours. I asked him if he was in the park alone, and he told me that his mom was in their apartment, down the block but out of sight and earshot of the park. Later I heard him discussing with his playmates how much he hated school, and I thought about the contrast between his freedom out of school and his confinement in the classroom. I wondered at the enormous self-discipline he would have to show in most classrooms, where his behavior and language would be continually scrutinized by a teacher. Small-group work helps a child like this to taste within the classroom's four walls a bit of the independence that he has out of school.

Another reason to master use of cooperative learning is to help students who are not native speakers of English learn both the new language and the content. Small-group work provides far more opportunities for kids to express themselves in a low-risk setting. They have a chance to practice English with native speakers, something they may not do outside school. Whole-class instruction simply doesn't give them the chance to use their new language frequently enough and in enough different ways. In addition, the anonymous, impersonal atmosphere of the urban school can be alienating to students who come from cultures in which teachers know and are familiar with families; small-group work, by helping students to develop relationships with one another, aids them in bridging the gap between the warmth and familiarity of home and the coldness and isolation of most urban schools.

The other reason I encourage you to learn how to use small groups well with your students is that when they are used correctly, they alter your students' relations with one another. Urban schools, especially the high schools, are frequently large and anonymous. Just as you don't have an opportunity to get to know your students if your contact with them is limited to your being in front of the class feeding them information, they don't have an opportunity to become acquainted with one another and develop the social and language skills people need to collaborate. We know from research that small-group work is one of the most effective strategies teachers can use to promote better intergroup relations among students, in the classroom specifically and in the school generally. One bonus of well-planned small groups is that they free up a few minutes for teachers to work with students individually. In the large classes that are common in urban schools, teachers have no time to work with students singly unless they find a way to create it.

In the years I've been supervising student teachers, I've encountered city teachers who tell me that group work is fine for some students, perhaps those in honors classes or the suburbs, but for "these kids," it's not an effective method of instruction. Opposition to small-group work frequently arises when the teacher does not know how to use the small group configuration appropriately or how to assess student work so that everyone learns. Often students have not been taught the social and language skills they need to work in groups. We're not born knowing how to collaborate; we acquire the knowledge and ability, either directly through instruction, or indirectly by observing and modeling behavior, or both. To use cooperative learning effectively, teachers have to analyze what academic and social skills their students need to know to accomplish the tasks set out for them. Then teachers have to teach these skills, just as they do content knowledge.

Small groups can be used to help students analyze hot topics without the risk that's incurred in commenting on a controversial issue in front of the entire class. Discussing racial, religious, and gender divisions in urban schools is especially difficult because teachers aren't given any institutional support for this tricky business. Although each of the three city high schools I taught in was troubled by overt bias against gays and racial or ethnic divisions among both staff and students, the schools never addressed the problems openly. My use of small groups helped students become sufficiently acquainted and comfortable with one another that we could discuss social tensions without the explosions that I and other teachers feared.

Cooperative learning helps integrate special education students into the classroom for all the reasons that it's beneficial for other students. In addition, when students are working with one another in well-planned small-group activities, you have a chance to circulate among the groups, providing extra assistance to students who require it. Many times your "special needs" students won't require help from you because their peers provide it—and benefit in the process, both socially and intellectually.

Of course, there are other valuable teaching strategies that you need to learn because you need to have a wide range of instructional alternatives at your fingertips. And I have to admit that I do know a few teachers who are highly respected and admired among students, faculty, and administrators who never use cooperative learning. They transmit their great love of learning and of the content, as well as their respect for each student, through their powerful personalities. However, for each teacher who succeeds brilliantly using an exclusive diet of whole-class instruction, I can point to 20 who don't. Moreover, there's no way we can duplicate the success of these remarkably talented teachers, except by cloning their personalities, whereas almost everyone can learn how to use small groups well.

Knowing the Subject Matter

The other indispensable ability for urban teachers is understanding their subject matter well enough to examine it from different perspectives. Here again the proficiency is one all teachers should have but urban teachers *must* have. Urban teachers need this skill more than teachers whose classrooms are less culturally diverse and filled with students who are confident of their ability to use schooling to improve their lives—and are therefore willing to put up with classes they find boring. When you are given a curriculum you have to follow or a textbook you must use, you need to know the subject well enough so that you can distill the essence of the material and then use your knowledge of teaching and your students' interests to present the concept or skill so that it's meaningful to your students. One of my student teachers described this process as being able to "walk around" the material, seeing it from other perspectives, so that he could reshape it for his students.

Whether you're teaching algebra, addition, Chaucer, or geography, you need to be able to answer this question: "Why am I teaching this content to these students?" If your response is that "It's in the curriculum" or "It's in the textbook" or "They need it for 5th grade," you've not acquired an understanding of the value of the content. You won't be able to make it meaningful to your students, so you'll be chained to an instructional routine that emphasizes rote learning and low-level cognitive skills. If the material is boring to you, you won't make it engaging for your students. As I discuss in the next chapter, creating high-quality lessons is the key to having your classroom function well; understanding the content you demand that your students master is key in planning interesting lessons.

Too often, because of pressures to improve standardized test scores, you must ask your students to study material that has little redeeming value other than its probable presence on a standardized test that affects their careers and yours as well. How can you deal with this pressure? If students have thrived for much of the year on stimulating content, they will usually stay focused for short intervals on material they find boring or skills that require drill. So one aim is to limit the amount of time you spend on test preparation as much as you possibly can. I suggest that you be frank about the reasons you are presenting content, separating material that you are being told to teach for test preparation from the work you truly find meaningful. In order to ask students to master content that they find irrelevant and boring, you need to have helped them to trust you and to have experienced a different kind of learning. To accomplish that end, you need to understand your students and the content you're teaching well enough to construct lessons that are motivating most of the time.

This strategy is more difficult in some subjects and some schools than others. Much depends on the degree to which content is controlled by forces outside your classroom. In some schools, principals and district supervisors scrutinize every student's test results and assume that if students have not done well, the teacher is at fault and the solution is more "test prep." In exceptional schools, the test results are used as the test makers say they should be, for diagnostic purposes. Teachers learn how to analyze the results and receive them in enough time to help individual kids improve. Another factor is that some subjects are taught in a strict sequence. If kids don't master a skill or concept at a particular moment, they'll be lost in the subsequent material. In situations like this, your ability to present concepts in many different ways is critical; your room to manipulate *what* you're teaching is quite limited, so you have to search for alternatives to teach the same material.

I hope my description of what you'll need to know does not imply that there are easy solutions. Kelly, a new teacher I interviewed for a research project, observed that in one way her education classes had led her astray. She remarked that "you learn to do a little of this, a little of that, and throw in some group work, and everything will be fine. But actually the kids are bouncing off of the walls and you don't know what to do! Nothing seems to work!" Kelly's criticism comes to my mind as I conclude this section because I think that my suggestions may be taken as recipes that will eliminate the intense frustrations and disappoint-ments that are an inevitable aspect of your life in the urban classroom. As an antidote to that impression, I'll share with you that in my sixth year of teaching in the city, I had a freshman English class after lunch that was impossible for me teach. It wasn't an especially large group, but it contained several young men who were 18 and 19 and visited class a day or two every few weeks, as well as a core of typical 14-year-olds, in-cluding four who had significant difficulties with English. I spent about half of every period reprimanding students for tossing books, calling out insults at one another, or grabbing some body part of a classmate. Just as I'd have some success in handling the 14-year-olds, one of the older students would come to class, completely out of the loop. I con-sulted counselors, and the department head; I revised the curriculum. Honestly, it was hell, and I said things to students I regretted as soon as the words left my mouth.

I've thought many times about that class, guiltily, trying to figure out what I could have done differently. I'm still not positive, but I think I might have saved that class by tracking down each of the young men who attended irregularly and developing an entirely individual course of study for him. But even that might not have worked because they missed whole weeks of all their classes, not only mine, so I needed to find something that was powerful enough to bring them to school, not just to my class.

We all have those classes, those days, or those weeks. In the next chapter I analyze the special problems of classroom management in ur-ban schools because I think that information will help you to reduce the number of times you feel like you'd rather be anywhere else, *anywhere*, but your classroom. Still, Kelly's final words remind us why, even after a class from hell, we stick it out and try harder.

"And then," she said, "you do something right and they learn. And you can see that they appreciate it. And there's no better feeling in the world."

7 Managing Your Classroom

If you're anxious about making your students do what you tell them to do, you're typical of most prospective and beginning teachers. "Discipline" and "class control" are often the greatest concerns novice teachers have, especially those who are not parents and have not worked in schools in other capacities. Young teachers going into urban schools who have not lived in the communities their school serves can be more apprehensive about managing the class if they have little experience with the neighborhood or the kids. In fact, the concern is well founded. An unfamiliarity with students as they are outside the school is a major hurdle to becoming comfortable and skillful in managing a city classroom. And though teachers may find admitting these feelings painful, in all honesty many have to acknowledge that they are fearful of their students and the setting.

I see this fear when I tell many educated, European American, middle-class people who have no personal contact with urban schools or minority children that I help prepare teachers for city schools. The response is frequently a jocular comment about whether I'm an expert in self-defense or use of lethal weapons. I attribute the comments partly to the portrait of urban schools and their students the media convey to the public. This caricature, combined with a lack of first-hand knowledge of urban classrooms and children, can heighten a prospective urban teacher's fears about kids' manageability and violence in schools. The fear exacerbates the usual apprehension about managing a classroom of people. We see news coverage of violence in schools so often that it's easy to assume they are like war zones. In my experience, the reality is quite different, although there's no doubt in my mind that urban teachers deal with the threat of violent behavior more often than do their counterparts in suburbs and small towns, and they have to be more knowledgeable and skillful in managing student behavior.

To some extent urban teaching's greater demand for skill in classroom management derives from the conditions I've described in this book: Chronic shortages of materials and supplies, poor facilities, isolation from parents and community, and bureaucratic intrusions and overregulation increase the difficulty of making the classroom a community and dealing with students as individuals. However, the surroundings in which city kids live also make establishing a respectful, focused classroom environment in an urban school a weighty challenge. Life in too many neighborhoods in American cities, especially the poorest sections, is more dangerous and anonymous than everyday existence in many other places. When I vacation in rural spots, I'm struck by customs that by city standards are foolishly naive: People leave bicycles unlocked on their porches, and farm stands are frequently left unattended, with customers trusted to leave money for the produce they take with them. When I dine in restaurants outside cities, I'm struck by the sight of women's purses dangling on the backs of their chairs, a habit that city-wise people regard as an invitation to theft.

Urban teachers have to know how to deal with the attitudes and habits that city kids acquire in their neighborhoods and homes because students bring behaviors grounded in their lives outside school into classrooms. Life is harsh for many city children, even those who experience bountiful family love and support. I'll never forget my dismay the first time I gave students in my English classes at Martin Luther King Jr. High School the same journal topic I had used in the suburbs, "A night I'll never forget." I was used to reading lighthearted anecdotes, tales of dates and family reunions, or perhaps a rueful recounting of an adolescent escapade that had ended with a minor punishment; on rare occasions a student would describe a very sad incident, like the death of a sibling or a parent. But in my classes at King the topic often generated stunning reports of friends lost to violent deaths, or one I'll never forget: A 15-year-old recalled attending the wake of her cousin, who had been killed by gunfire; what stuck in her mind was not the wake, but the theft of the gold chain from her cousin's corpse.

Kids who grow up in poor neighborhoods are often surrounded by brutal crime, and the behavior that helps them to survive in their neighborhood often conflicts with the deportment schools and teachers demand. In a classroom we require students to replace a defensive stance and aggressive behavior with quite a different sort of conduct. We insist that they negotiate differences and rely on school authorities to protect their personal safety, rather than defending themselves as they must do outside the school walls. As I described earlier in the coats-in-the-classroom problem, urban schools often don't adequately safeguard students and their property. When schools and teachers demand that students follow regulations that make them vulnerable but do not simultaneously offer a safe environment, they inadvertently encourage children to disregard and reject the school's behavioral norms. Children often violate school rules of conduct, sacrificing their prospect of academic success, to safeguard themselves and their belongings because they do not trust authorities in schools to provide them with adequate protection. You need to make your classroom a safe haven so that your students don't have to choose between protecting their person and property or conforming to classroom norms.

Like most teacher educators, I don't advise you to think about the task of making your classroom orderly, safe, and productive simply in terms of disciplining students to make them do what you want or controlling their misbehavior. If you want your students to act differently in your classroom than they do on the street, you need to be proactive in establishing a classroom environment that supports the behaviors you demand. You need to make classroom rules and policies explicit, explain their value, teach them, and reinforce them all the time. All aspects of classroom life should encourage appropriate behavior and discourage conduct that makes other students feel devalued or unsafe. No matter how much or how severely you discipline students, you won't have a well-functioning classroom if the setup undercuts or contradicts the stated rules. For example, you may tell your students in no uncertain terms that they are not to play with the special materials you will distribute to them until *after* you've given them directions for the project. However, if you pass out the materials—whether it's paint, candies, microscopes, or tape recorders—*before* you give instructions, you've invited misbehavior by prolonging the amount of time students have to refrain from using these seductive materials. The procedure you've used to organize the lesson undercuts the behavior you want from the students, and when Clarisse, Eddy, and Frank fool with the microscopes, you have to halt instruction to discipline them. However, if you had anticipated the problem and distributed the materials *after* you had given instructions for the project, you would have helped everyone to focus on the instructions, not the materials. Using the concept of "classroom management" helps you to shift your focus from incidents of misbehavior to an examination of everything that occurs in the classroom in order to support rather than undercut the behavior you want to elicit.

As you're thinking through the rules that you believe must guide life in the classroom community, you first need to examine your expectations critically. Is the behavior you demand truly essential for your students? Why? Is the conduct you're insisting on a cultural norm you've simply imported from your own education, or is it a crucial skill the children you work with need to succeed academically? I sometimes see teachers expending considerable energy on enforcing ritual behavior, like having their students fold their hands on their desks or rise to say "Good morning" in unison to visitors. However, when asked the reason for this required behavior, the children can't explain. On the other hand, I worked with a teacher who insisted on formalities such as rising to greet visitors to reinforce social etiquette, which she defined as treating other people with respect and consideration. "Having good manners" in her classroom meant being respectful to her and to classmates, and she linked etiquette to academic norms she wanted to reinforce as well as to behaviors students might have been taught at home. So if students interrupted or insulted one another the teacher admonished them for having "poor manners" and reminded them of the reasons "good manners" were expected in her classroom.

Once you clarify your expectations, you should make sure that your students understand the purpose of the behaviors you expect because the behavior may contradict what they've been told at home or learned from experience. If you defend a prohibition against fighting by telling your students "Fighting is wrong," but they know they must defend themselves with their fists if they're attacked in the park, you're undermining your own legitimacy. In order to succeed in school, students whose culture contrasts sharply with European American, middle-class norms must learn to live in two cultures that require different ways of talking and acting. You can help them by clarifying the differences and similarities, rather than assuming and insisting that the school's norms are always superior. So instead of saying "Fighting is wrong," and thereby implying that putting up a struggle when someone tries to steal their bike is wrong, you can say that "We don't fight in the classroom," explaining why. Even young children can engage in fruitful analysis of standards for judging when fighting is prudent, necessary, and ethical; as a bonus, this discussion will teach you much about your students' world and values, data you'll find helpful in refining—or perhaps modifying—your case for the behavior you insist on in your classroom.

You may have to teach your students social and academic skills that you take for granted and that you assume they know, for instance, bringing supplies to class, being quiet when classmates perform, or negotiating a dispute rather than hitting or hurling insults. You and I were not born knowing these behaviors that support academic learning.

Someone, somewhere taught us that when a classmate is speaking, we should not and that when the teacher writes notes on the board, that's a cue that it's important information, even if she or he does not tell students to take it down. If we want to have a well-functioning classroom, we have to assume the job of teaching kids what they need to succeed in our class. Ideally, instruction in social skills is integrated into material you'd teach anyhow, but sometimes you have to make instructional detours to help all kids reach the destination.

Excellent urban teachers use a wide range of teaching strategies to help their students learn and practice appropriate social interaction in classrooms, and to make your classroom a well-functioning community, you'll have to become adept at these techniques—and quickly. One key is to model the behaviors that you expect. If you don't want students to shout at one another, be late, or be rude, then you cannot either. A strategy I've seen teachers at all grade levels use successfully to help students practice behaviors that are new and feel awkward is having them role-play a scenario that evokes strong reactions and conflict. Students experience acting differently in an imagined situation before they are expected to act this way during the classroom's normal functioning.

If you're reading this book as part of a college course to prepare you to teach, you may have heard the axiom that well-planned lessons are the heart of effective classroom management. That's even truer in urban schools because the school has procedures and policies that undercut your ability to make class engaging. Countless times I gnashed my teeth when my class was interrupted and the students' attention span broken by an inane announcement on the public address system or a student courier bringing a form I had to fill out because a deadline loomed (or had passed) for the administration to submit papers to a regulatory agency. Another distraction to school is . . . life! Recent social, political, and economic changes in our society, especially increased job insecurity and cuts to social programs, have put enormous stress on children and families. Even middle-class families find that parents' job and personal commitments make children's school lives difficult to oversee, and kids are under considerably more pressure to succeed in school than they were just a generation ago. Kids experience numerous situations outside school that make concentrating on academics a tough challenge. Some children have home lives that are unsafe or insecure, emotionally and physically. For other students, especially adolescents, the financial rewards that we assume accompany academic achievement seem (and, in fact, may be) unobtainable:

What's the use of going to school if you know dozens of high school grads who can't find a decent-paying job?

When we focus only on the problems in families or poor neighborhoods, we miss the ways that schools themselves sabotage kids' enthusiasm for learning and their school achievement. One policy that often makes kids feel that they cannot be successful in school is "ability grouping," or "tracking," which reinforces students' lack of confidence in themselves as learners. Although most American schools divide students according to what is said to be their "ability," the policy is probably most fully developed in large urban districts.

Before teaching in the New York City schools, I wasn't convinced that kids' self-image was influenced by tracking. In retrospect, I think I missed the cues the kids sent me in the suburban schools because the racial and class differences among the tracks were more muted than they are in urban school systems. For instance, some schools in New York City still place kids in classes that are labeled chronologically to denote "ability." If you are a 7th grader in "7-1" you know you are hot stuff. But if you are a "7-12" in a school having 12 7th-grade homerooms, you know you are in the cellar (figuratively and sometimes literally as well). I learned how much the process of tracking affects kids' view of themselves when I listened to my students at both King and Humanities discuss the process for "selecting" high schools. My students at King, a neighborhood school that enrolled all students in the zone who wanted to attend it, chafed at the presence of LaGuardia High School of Music & Art and Performing Arts in a building across the street. They viewed kids from LaGuardia, which has a highly competitive entrance procedure, as privileged; fights often broke out between students in the two schools. A few years later, when I asked a class of students at Humanities High School—like King, a school without selective admissions—why they had chosen the school, one girl called out that no one in Humanities was smart enough to get into Stuyvesant or Bronx High School of Science or LaGuardia. Sadly, not one student in the class contradicted her statement—or the implication that at the age of 14 they were already losers.

We know from much research that the lower tracks contain a disproportionate number of students who are working-class African American and Hispanic, who are rarely exposed to instruction that calls for high-level cognition, creativity, or choice. These students, whose expectations for themselves mirror the school's minimal expectations, often feel too defeated to even attempt schoolwork. When they are in low tracks in schools that are racially segregated, their feeling of being rejected is almost overwhelming, and they often express their feelings of self-defeat and hopelessness with amazing candor. It's not unusual to hear kids in the lowest tracks make comments like "We don't do much work 'cause we're in the dumb class." Tracking takes many forms, as my examples indicate. Classes, programs, and entire schools may be tracked. I should note that there are thoughtful, dedicated teachers who defend the use of "tracks" as the best way to help kids get the specialized attention they need. Though I disagree with them, I think there is consensus that the best teachers help kids to see beyond the labels, to understand that the labels need not be accepted as destiny.

Dealing with School Violence

Beyond excellent classroom management skills that help you keep violent disputes from developing, the key to dealing with violent behavior in the classroom is to know your students and respect them. Consider this: In the years that I taught in New York City, I worked with about 2,000 teenagers, many of them from violent neighborhoods, yet I dealt with only one I felt was dangerous. Most of the time when I heard about an incident in which a student physically assaulted a teacher, I knew from my own dealings with the teacher that she or he treated students inhumanely, abusing the teacher's authority—for instance, by reading test scores aloud to embarrass students who had failed or by ridiculing them. Here again let me draw a distinction between justifying behavior and explaining it. The behavior of students who assault or threaten teachers (or classmates) can't be justified or tolerated. But what's often overlooked in these situations is that the behavior could have been short-circuited had the teacher been more reflective.

If you treat your students with empathy, consideration, and respect, you need not fear them. With most students, violent behavior is a response to a perceived provocation, not a random act, so if you avert confrontations, you avoid violence. Many poor city kids live with a degree of stress and pressure that gives them hair-trigger tempers, and teachers have to keep this is mind when addressing misbehavior. Obviously you don't pursue a disagreement with someone who seems to be on the brink of exploding, even if you are angry yourself. As the adult with authority, you have to step away from the confrontation so that it doesn't escalate. I'd often tell an angry student, "We can talk about that after class, in private," so that I retained my authority in front of the class but avoided further conflict. Often the privacy did indeed permit us to negotiate a mutually acceptable settlement.

The most frightening news reports often describe students who bring weapons to school. The experiences I've had with students who've brought weapons to school illustrate that even this extreme case doesn't necessarily demonstrate that a student is dangerous or a criminal. In my first year of teaching in New York City, Danny, a student in my first-period class, was suspended for carrying a knife in school. I was more than a little frightened thinking about how Danny, who attended class irregularly, might have used the knife on me or a classmate. As I eavesdropped on a conversation between two colleagues, one of whom had taught Danny in previous years, I heard the situation cast differently. Danny, who was large for his 15 years, took the subway to his full-time job in a distant, dangerous section of the Bronx every day after school. He worked from 3:00 P.M. to 11:00 P.M., six days a week, to support his siblings and infirm mother. Because he had to be at work promptly at 3:00 P.M. for the shift change, on schooldays he had no time to go home to pick up the knife, which he needed for protection coming home late at night. A teacher who spotted the knife when it fell out of Danny's pocket, as Danny bent over in the hallway to pick up a dropped book, notified a security guard. Danny was automatically suspended, per the new zero-tolerance policy put into effect in response to publicity about unsafe schools.

After his suspension, Danny returned to class for a few sessions. We had not developed much of relationship because he was very seldom in class, but the information I had learned about his full-time job made me look on him differently. I took an opportunity when he was in class shortly after the suspension to ask why he was usually absent. He explained that he had to help his younger siblings get ready for school and that he was often too tired to wake up an hour earlier so that he'd have time to shower and eat himself in time for first period. Until that point, I had never known anyone who regularly carried a weapon, and I realized that I didn't know what I would have done in Danny's situation, especially since he received no help in shouldering the adult burden of supporting his family while simultaneously trying to finish high school. Although the prohibition against carrying weapons in school was certainly justified, the school never addressed the reasons students violated the regulation. Had the school environment been less anonymous and inflexible and had counselors been available, Danny could have received help in dealing with his problem. For instance, he might have been given a reduced class schedule, to allow him to come later to school and leave earlier. Another possibility would have been to try to find him a job closer to school and his home, to pare down time lost in his commute. In both cases he would not have needed to bring the knife to school and would have averted the suspension.

The incident with Danny proved to be a dress rehearsal for a situation I confronted later that year when Sonya, an outspoken, hot-tempered young woman in one of my classes, emptied her purse on a table while searching for an elusive pen. A penknife tumbled out, along with various lipsticks, nail polish, and key chains. Sonya immediately noticed that I had seen the knife and apologized profusely for her indiscretion. When I told her that she shouldn't have the knife in school, she admonished me, saying something like, "You think I'm crazy, to go in the elevator in my building without something to protect me? *You* be there in that dark elevator and hallway with nobody around. You think I'm going to let some joker rape or murder me without no fight?"

In a grim tone of voice, I reminded Sonya that she couldn't have the knife in school without risking suspension and told her to put it away and never let me see it again. I could understand why a colleague might feel obligated to report the incident, and I worried that if Sonya felt physically threatened in school she might use the knife. But I also knew that Sonya faced a dilemma that the school ignored. As was the case with Danny, the school provided Sonya with no help in dealing with the real dangers she faced. Why were there no counselors in the school with connections to security officials in the projects? Who was available in the school to help Sonya come up with another solution? If reporting her would result in her receiving help, then it made sense. But all that I'd accomplish by enforcing the policy would be to further alienate Sonya from school and teachers. I was certain that if she was suspended, she would either drop out of school or return and continue to carry the knife because nothing else would have changed. I decided to not report the incident; instead, I talked with her about how she might get home safely without bringing a knife to school—and crossed my fingers that she would never use the knife in school.

Another incident occurred when I was teaching at King, a few years later. I saw a student I knew only by sight display a gun to others who had gathered in the hallway outside my room, between classes. He observed my glance and quickly hid the gun in his jacket pocket. I raced to call security using the closest phone, in the departmental office, which had been locked as usual by the chairperson, Mr. X. Unable to call, I asked a colleague passing by to contact security with the message that

I had seen a student carrying a gun. Eventually the gun, which was not loaded, was found in a locker and confiscated; the student was suspended. However, the incident greatly alarmed me, and for days I worried that the student would retaliate against me for reporting him.

In both situations students violated a policy that made sense, yet I responded differently. The nature of the violations differed in that Sonya had a penknife and the other student a gun, but on reflection, I think that my reaction was also due to the context of confronting violence. I had a relationship with Sonya and therefore I wasn't frightened by her, though her behavior disturbed me. In the other predicament, I was terrified because the student was a stranger to me. I think these incidents illustrate that as soon as your students become people to you, your decisions about punishment and discipline change; but you can deal with your students as human beings and individuals only if you are not afraid of them, and racial and class differences frequently make us fear people with whom we have no personal relations.

One of the reasons I strongly advise that prospective urban teachers become comfortable with the kinds of students they're going to be teaching before they assume a position of authority, even as a student teacher, is that when we can see our students as human beings like ourselves rather than as "the other," we can separate the person from the act and intervene appropriately. When I spotted Sonya's knife, I was scared because I'm not accustomed to being with people who carry weapons and know that their presence dramatically escalates the risks of bodily harm in arguments. However, I wasn't as afraid of Sonya, and therefore I could analyze, rationally, how best to handle the situation. On the other hand, when I saw the student displaying a gun in the hallway, I feared him and the behavior because I didn't know him personally. In retrospect, I think my apprehension about retribution was inflated by the social gulf of race and class. Sonya was a Puerto Rican female; the male with the gun was African American.

On occasion I've been able to explore these two incidents with experienced urban teachers in a racially and socially mixed class. My students and I have had some wonderfully candid, thoughtful discussions about how race and gender affect our interactions with students. In one particularly frank session, I shared the following experience to help us think through the implications of racial differences between teachers and students. When I returned to King High School as a visitor after teaching college for several years, I found myself frightened at the sea of noisy Black teenagers flooding out of the building at the end of the day. As I grappled with my anxiety, I recalled that I had felt the same way on the first few weeks teaching there. The feeling wore off without my noticing it was gone, and I had forgotten it entirely until it returned after my long absence. I remembered that when I taught at King some of my European American friends had expressed their apprehension at being around crowds of Black teenagers and had wondered aloud to me why I wasn't afraid.

Most of the African American teachers in my college class, mothers and fathers of teenagers, made comments that showed that they were either bemused or offended that anyone would find a crowd of Black teenagers frightening. The European American teachers, most of whom taught in schools in which White students were a minority, did not enter into the conversation, so I don't know what they were thinking. I struggled to answer the question of what had frightened me, what would scare middle-aged European Americans, about being with Black teenagers. Then Mildred, a middle-aged African American woman raised in a small town in the South, related an anecdote that revealed a similar response—to White teenagers. Mildred was driving her daughter home from college late at night and decided to save time by exiting from the highway on an unfamiliar road that took her through a nearby White working-class community. On this warm June night, she saw a large cluster of young White males, sitting on their cars and the sidewalks, drinking beer and shouting to one another. She was panic-stricken, fearing for her daughter and her safety as she stopped for a red light; and she hit the accelerator as hard as she could when the light changed. Mildred and I agreed that if I had been in her situation and she in mine, neither of us would have been frightened.

For both of us, the feeling of racial isolation in a group we regarded as "the other" provoked a deep fear. I think for many young, European American teachers, the same occurs when they begin their careers in racially segregated schools. They fear their students but are ashamed to admit it, and even if they could find someone to talk with, which they can't, they would not. Our society is supposed to be based on ideals of racial and social equality, and acknowledging that our behavior contradicts those ideals can be humiliating. We live in a society that is racially segregated, and few people have friends of different races with whom they talk about race frankly. To make matters worse, the culture in most schools makes pointed discussion of race almost a taboo, especially when the teaching staff and students differ in their race, for instance, when teachers are predominantly European American and the students,

African American. As some interesting research indicates, even when teachers are explicitly committed to working through racial divisions, to creating "safe spaces" to analyze attitudes about race, the lack of models about how to navigate this new territory is a daunting challenge.

When teachers are intimidated by their students, they're unable to address problem behavior straightforwardly because their fear is paralyzing. In my experience working with new teachers who are afraid of their students but unwilling to admit it, the strategy most adopt is to ignore the misconduct. But all of a teacher's words and actions are educative, and when teachers consistently disregard students' inappropriate behavior, they're actually sending a message to the unruly student that the conduct will be accepted. Children know when teachers fear them and resent it because the fear is demeaning in its reversal of appropriate adult–child relations. The misbehaving child is not receiving suitable guidance from the adult in authority, and the child realizes it, perhaps more quickly than the adult.

Establishing Your Moral Authority

The options a teacher has to punish misconduct are quite limited. After all, the most draconian punishments, like striking children or expelling them, can't be exercised often, even when they're legal. Though historians have demonstrated that disruptive students are not a new phenomena, I think the problem of establishing control in the classroom is a greater challenge today.

One enormous change is that for the first time in our history as a nation, American society is legally committed to providing *all* children with equal educational opportunities. Before the civil rights movement succeeded in eliminating legally sanctioned segregation, before bilingual and special education became legal requirements, if students were viewed as troublesome, they were excluded from schools. In addition, Americans who did not need education to overcome racial discrimination didn't need much formal schooling because decent-paying work didn't require academic credentials. Teachers today have to know how to teach types of kids whom American society has never before attempted to educate, yet schooling's organization has not changed to accommodate this challenge.

I often hear new teachers, especially those who have attended parochial schools with classmates who shared a similar cultural background, angrily recall that "When I was growing up, I did what the teacher said, or *else!*" They are stunned and frustrated that as teachers their decisions aren't automatically obeyed. What they have to consider is that as public school teachers, they have an obligation to work with *all* students, including the sort who were expelled from the private schools they attended—or restricted by de facto residential segregation from attending their suburban public schools. Also, many parochial schools have an explicit moral vision that parents must endorse and that the school promotes. The teacher is given her authority by the institution, which parents trust and support.

Years ago, teachers could rely more on the power of their position, or what is called their "uniformed authority," to impose their will in the classroom. Their role as teacher gave them a significant degree of control, just as the police officer's uniform (even without the holster) confers power. Immigrant parents and students who have not yet assumed this society's dominant values and come from countries in which only a tiny proportion of the population is educated beyond basic literacy and numeracy often display a respect for the teacher's uniformed authority: Regardless of how well or poorly teachers perform, they are highly respected, even revered; the teacher's word is almost never disputed. However, when the teacher's uniformed authority is rejected or challenged, as it is among students and families who are mistrustful of schools because of society's failure to include them as equals, the teacher has to rely on two other sources of control: *moral* and *technical* authority.

People exert technical authority when their clients believe them to be far more expert than themselves about the service being rendered. We don't generally question the doctor's diagnosis because we acknowledge that the doctor has access to knowledge and skills that we don't. As with uniformed authority, technical authority is of relatively little value to urban teachers, in part because so many aspects of what and how to teach are disputed. Although researchers have developed some broad agreement about "best practices," there are important discrepancies that aren't erased by local, state, or federal regulations to use one approach or another. Classroom teachers know all too well that teaching materials and methods mandated today because "the research" shows they are best are often tossed out the window in 5 years because a contradictory approach based on "the research" has been demonstrated to be superior. Another limitation to technical authority is that students or parents who are suspicious of whether school people have the students' best interests at heart are not likely to be convinced to do as the teacher says because of his or her superior knowledge of the subject area or teaching.

Urban teachers' primary source of control is their "moral" authority, which rests on the perception of students and parents that the teacher is knowledgeable about the subject matter, competent in pedagogy, and committed to helping all students succeed, in school and life. As I've stressed throughout this book, although a teacher's deeds may be proof positive to him or her of dedicated performance, students and parents may have a contradictory perception. I learned this the hard way when I unknowingly offended an African American student in one of my classes at Humanities High School with a jocular reprimand I made to a classmate. The remark was a stock comment I had used many times at King, to what I thought was my students' great pleasure, and I was stunned and hurt that my remark could be taken as racist. After some painful reflection, I realized that my remark was indeed insensitive and that certain teaching behaviors that seemed to serve me well at King were perceived differently by the more middle-class student population at Humanities. In fact, there may have been King students who were offended but had not made their feelings known.

What you think is caring behavior may not be perceived as such by your students and their parents. Racial, gender, and class differences between teachers and students, power inequities in relationships, and the school's insularity all converge to make communication difficult, so disparate perceptions of actions are common. Establishing your moral authority depends on your ability to view your own performance from your students' and their parents' eyes. Remember Mrs. M, who carried armloads of practice exams home to correct? That's a perfect example of an action that to some teachers is clear evidence of dedication; but to many of her students Mrs. M was simply forcing them to do yet another tedious exercise, exercising her power as the teacher. Her reminders about the importance of the exam were taken as scolding.

As I learned from the fallout from my joke that offended a student, there's no formula for ensuring that your performance will be perceived as you intend it. However, the more conscious you are of the problems caused by the classroom's isolation from parents and community—of the ways suspicions are fed by disparities in gender, race, and class—the more capable you'll be of establishing classroom routines and methods of dealing with your students that convey your dedication and win their trust. Your moral authority is based on your ability to demonstrate to your students and their parents that in your role as teacher you intend to assist each of your students—and that you are capable of doing so. When you make instruction engaging and worthwhile and when you establish a classroom environment that is based on mutual respect, you establish your moral authority, which gives you more control and authority than the threat or use of punishment.

This may seem hopelessly idealistic or Pollyanna-ish to some readers, so I hope the following example from my experience will persuade you differently. Unlike most high school teachers, I always enjoyed decorating my classroom and keeping art supplies on hand for special projects. I noticed that few city teachers kept anything more than a pencil in their desks, even when they didn't travel between classrooms and had a room of their own. I was told that nothing was safe unless it was locked up, including pens and pencils. One or two people told me not to decorate my room because posters would be vandalized or stolen. I decided that I couldn't work in an environment of such mistrust, but on the other hand, I knew that leaving expensive equipment, like my small tape recorder, in an unlocked place would create an unnecessary temptation.

I decided to act as I had throughout my previous years of teaching. I locked up in a closet all the items of significant value, like my purse and electronic equipment and the class set of pocket dictionaries I had bought with my own money. Everything else, including my prized art pencils and desk supplies, stayed in my desk. In addition, I usually kept a few dollars in change in an envelope in the top drawer, to buy raffles or make donations when students were collecting for a worthwhile cause. As I had in the suburbs, I decorated my classroom walls with art and movie posters I knew the students would like, as well as displays of their work. The only action I took that was different from what I done before was that I made the reasons for my actions explicit. I concluded that if other teachers were not decorating their rooms, students might not realize what behaviors I expected from them. In other words, I had to teach some social skills that were needed for the classroom to function as I wanted. On the first day of class, when I introduced myself to the students, I asked them to look around the room and tell me how they felt about the posters, plants, and decorations. Students remarked that they disliked the "boring" (their word) sterility (my word) of most classrooms and enjoyed working in a room that looked more like a home. I explained that I had spent my money and time improving the room's appearance so that we could all enjoy being in an environment that made us feel better about ourselves. And just as we expect respect and consideration for our belongings when we invite someone into our home, I expected my students to treat my decorations and property respectfully. To be certain that my expectations were clear, I described the behavior I wanted: No one would go into my desk without asking; no one would write on or deface anything on the walls; anyone who borrowed materials would return them in the same condition they were in when taken. In return, I would continue to make sure the room was a pleasant working space for us.

In my 7 subsequent years of city teaching, only once was anything taken from my desk (the money, when I was on jury duty) or a decoration vandalized during class (again, when I was on jury duty). Although I generally circulated around the room during class and seldom sat at my desk, I didn't worry that students would steal supplies from it, and they did not. My trust in them was rewarded, as yours will be if you exercise your authority with concern for their self-respect, dignity, and sense of earned accomplishment, with attention to the human needs and desires we all share.

8 Your Moral and Political Obligations

After reading my descriptions of the problems you'll face as an urban teacher, you may be rethinking your decision to teach in an urban school. I can hear some of my friends who are career teachers say, "Everything you've said is accurate; but, Lo, if you tell them all this, anyone who's sane won't want to teach in the city!" They have a point, and I'm reminded of what occurred during the Italian campaign in World War II when the Army commissioned a well-known filmmaker to create a documentary that would show soldiers what battle would be like: After showing it a few times, the Army suppressed the film because it terrified the soldiers it was supposed to inform.

Unlike soldiers who are drafted during war, city teachers enlist voluntarily, and I hope people won't take on the job if they haven't thought seriously about the demands that will be made on them and wrestled with their conscience about the extent to which they are willing to extend themselves to children they must serve. I've described the many ways in which teaching is a job and teachers are treated as workers, but teaching also has moral dimensions we associate with careers that we refer to as "callings." Every so often in my college classes, I come across new and prospective teachers whose stance toward teaching is that it's a job that's not so different from any other civil service position. They've decided that their responsibilities are clear-cut and that self-sacrifice is certainly not one of them. Frankly, I don't want people to become city teachers if they don't see that almost every day of their career they'll be making difficult decisions about how much they can and should do to help their students.

I've assumed in this book that you have already considered teaching's many satisfactions, but after all the negatives I've discussed, it probably can't hurt to remind you that I stayed an urban teacher because it was an exciting, satisfying occupation. Urban teaching is a tough job, but it also has wonderful rewards. In the years I was a city teacher, I loved my work. Its value was clear to me, and I was able to grow professionally. I changed what and how I taught with enough frequency to keep me puzzling over how best to present material or handle problems with kids and colleagues. Although testing pressures have increased, teachers in most urban schools still have a degree of autonomy that is envied by people in a corporate setting with supervisors peering over them in their cubicles.

Despite these rewards, it may seem like the job of teaching I've described is more than a person should be asked to handle for a lifetime, and indeed it may be. I know of only a handful of city teachers who have made a lifetime career of teaching and thrived in the classroom until they retired. Many more who remain in the classroom have ceased taking much pleasure from their work. I think that in most city schools serving the highest proportions of children from impoverished, violent neighborhoods, the conditions are so wearing that it's utopian to expect teachers to sustain their dedication and idealism for 30 years. Not too many children in these schools overcome the staggering social, economic, and educational barriers that impede academic achievement, and a similarly small number of dedicated teachers start and end their teaching careers in the most difficult schools with the same degree of enthusiasm and commitment with which they began. I suggest that you don't assume that you'll be doing the same job in three decades. You may enjoy teaching in a city school enormously after you become proficient, but after several years you may weary of the routine as well as of the disparity between what you're expected to do and the support that you're provided. It's unfair and educationally indefensible that city teachers are treated like disposable commodities, but they are, and at the start of this challenge you should be clear-eyed about what you've undertaken.

When teaching no longer provides you with a strong sense of satisfaction, when you feel worn out by the responsibility, it's time for you to intervene. The school system itself doesn't help teachers to renew themselves, so they must monitor and take charge of their professional and psychological well-being independently. To revitalize themselves, some teachers return to school for another degree, in a field related to teaching or another area they're considering as an alternative occupation. If it's possible, return to being a student yourself on a full-time basis so that you experience a total break from your life as a teacher. One friend takes unpaid leaves to travel the world whenever she can afford it and returns renewed. Another colleague took off a year to work in personnel and found that although she could easily earn more money in this occupation, she missed being in school; her year away helped her identify satisfactions about the job she hadn't previously noticed. A strategy many teachers use is to make a lateral move into another school-based occupation, such as counseling. Other teachers, like myself, leave K–12 teaching for the college level or careers in the private sector.

People who remain in the classroom when they no longer want to be there are among the most unhappy workers you'll ever meet. Teaching has modest rewards outside of the satisfaction that you've connected with your students; and when this pleasure diminishes for urban teachers, the negative aspects of the job become overwhelming. Two months off in the summer, job security, and a decent pension can't compensate for 10 months of feeling hostile toward and unappreciated by your students. The teachers who have convinced themselves that the job security they have makes their unhappiness acceptable don't generally persuade anyone else who knows them, least of all their students. When you start to identify the students as the source of your frustration, and the gratification you receive from your teaching doesn't compensate for the frustrations, change your career.

Some educational researchers and teacher educators write about the need for teachers to be "change agents" who take leadership in improving conditions in the school. This may be possible in small, innovative schools that have a high proportion of seasoned teachers and administrators with a shared vision, but in general I think learning to teach in urban schools is a job-and-a-half. Especially in the first years of urban teaching, most new teachers have little time or energy for anything beyond survival. Another problem with this change-agent strategy for reforming schools is that it focuses on the role of teachers as individuals, but urban teachers face a formidable bureaucracy, and more than one fine teacher has found that battling the school bureaucracy is a Promethean struggle.

Many of the best teachers feel that they satisfy their moral and professional obligations by serving their students well. They focus completely and wholeheartedly on their students' well-being and their teaching. Their professional lives, and sometimes their personal lives, too, are engaged with helping the children they teach. These teachers render invaluable service to the schools and their students; without their dedication, urban schools and the communities they serve would be far worse. Still, I encourage you to adopt an orientation toward school reform that moves beyond this singular focus on your own classroom and the students who absorb so much of your attention.

The conditions in urban schools that sabotage effective, engaging teaching and learning can be improved if teachers and their organizations assume greater political leadership for redirecting public discussion and policy about schools. There's not room here for me to enumerate the ways in which current debate and law are skewed, but I must briefly explain why the commonplace debate about choosing between "equity" and "excellence," between extending equal educational opportunity to all kids and maintaining high standards of achievement, is misleading. It presumes that we have to choose between these ideals because as a society we can't do both. I'd say there's no reason—other than the lack of political will to make the society more equitable—that we even should have this discussion. "Equity" has never been a reality in public education. Many groups of kids who were excluded from society's promise of an equal education have won a place in public schools because parents and advocacy groups agitated long and hard. Unfortunately, laws and regulations intended to help students who were previously ignored by public education are often conceptually flawed or poorly implemented. Programs to serve handicapped and second-language learners have been glued onto dysfunctional school systems. A colleague once described dealing with the New York City school system as being like wrestling with an octopus that has no head: It's not possible to escape the tentacles and it's also not possible to get at a nerve center. Though well intentioned, new programs are new tentacles, creating additional complications for already overextended classroom teachers.

When experienced city teachers in my graduate courses are asked to choose a subject for a research project that examines a thorny problem in their schools, most select topics related to second-language learners (ESL and bilingual programs) and inclusion or integration of special education students. The teachers discover, to their great surprise, that there are schools, usually ones in well-funded suburbs, that implement these programs well. They see that we know how to carry out these programs so that they improve education—for everyone. However, more often than not the form special programs take in city schools bears little resemblance to the models—except in name. The intent of the programs, to support kids who need special assistance, is often undercut by the way they are carried out. Teachers have students with severe disabilities and difficulty with English added to already overcrowded classrooms. Students and teachers fail to receive the supports and resources they need.

Some pundits and teachers argue that the reality of poor implementation of programs intended to increase educational opportunity proves that schools cannot or should not make accommodations for kids who fall outside the continuum of what schools regard as "normal." Another perspective, one you can hear from teachers who are successful with a wide range of kids, is that the programs are failing because we have not invested enough time and care to make them operate as they should. These teachers recall, either from personal experience or their reading of history, the unfair conditions that prompted creation of special programs. They observe that continuing prejudice makes academic success more elusive for city children born into poverty. Their refusal to accept the notion that as a society we must choose between equity and excellence informs their decisions about how to navigate the roadblocks set before urban teachers.

Urban teaching is undoubtedly tougher today than it was when I had my own classroom, but I faced, as you will, the "bottom line" of having responsibility for kids without being given the resources needed to do the job well. I know from experience how much more difficult teaching is when the classroom serves students who are labeled as having severe behavior problems and those who have significant physical handicaps. Martin Luther King Jr. High School was housed in a modern building that had elevators and was wheelchair-accessible, so we were one of the few Manhattan high schools that students in wheelchairs could attend. When my classes contained a student in a wheelchair, almost every aspect of teaching was harder, due to no fault of the handicapped student. The biggest problems were related to logistics, not teaching. For example, I made a point of stressing punctuality and began class when the bell rang. Because students from other classes stayed in the hallways and delayed going to classes to call out to their friends sitting in classrooms, I'd often have to lock the door shortly after the bell rang. Due to problems with the elevator or the bus that transported them, students in wheelchairs were often absent or very late. Their entry invariably created a disturbance because while the door was being held open, a student passing through the hall would beckon or insult someone in my class.

Perhaps you will be more patient and understanding than I was, but I had to struggle not to feel frustrated at having students in wheelchairs in my class because of the additional work their presence caused me. Yet it would be hard to find someone more sympathetic than I am to inclusion as an ideal because of my personal knowledge of what life was like for handicapped children before passage of legislation guaranteeing their educational opportunities. My younger sister is blind, and I recall clearly the sacrifices families had to make to educate their handicapped children. Children who were mentally retarded were frequently hidden at home and not educated at all; kids with physical handicaps had to begin attending boarding schools at a young age if their parents wanted them to receive any schooling. One of my sister's friends attended my junior high and high school, and her mother went with her to escort her from class to class and to take notes that she later Brailled. The family was responsible for obtaining, when they could, copies of books in Braille from the Library of Congress. The school had no responsibility to help—and didn't. Few of the dozen or so blind children my sister's age received more than a grade school education. Most have spent their lives virtually home-bound; a few work in sheltered workshops. Of the entire cohort, two or three live independently and work in regular jobs. I know firsthand how critically important the legislation expanding the nation's commitment to educational opportunity has been for tens of thousands of children.

When teachers in my college classes realize that add-on programs in their schools could be conceptualized and operated differently, their anger about the programs is often replaced by frustration. They see no way for programs like inclusion and bilingual education to work well unless urban schools are transformed: to encourage collaboration among parents, teachers, and administrators; to make time spent on professional development worthwhile; to alter school environments so that tolerance and understanding of cultural and social differences are expected. And so our class discussions about teaching and learning turn to discussions of what teachers can do to make these changes occur.

Teachers are often active as individuals in political and community groups, which is commendable, but we need to take another step. We have a special responsibility to educate the public about what's needed for all kids to have the education they deserve, primarily because teachers have access to insider knowledge of schools that parents and other citizens don't. The dangers confronting city schools extend far beyond the budget cutbacks of recent years that seem taken for granted by the public. Our government's responsibility to oversee and fund a system of public education, one that provides equal educational opportunity to everyone, is being questioned, even attacked, as are the actual gains made in the past 40 years to make the government live up to its responsibilities. Advocates for public education now battle schemes to use tax money to support private schools, testing pressures that reduce instruction in schools serving poor and working-class kids to little more than vocational training for menial jobs, regulations dictating what materials teacher can use to teach reading or sex education, and many other policies that enlarge the gulf between the education children in cities desperately need and the one they receive.

Unions are not often seen by new teachers as vehicles for progressive social change. In fact, unions are so much a part of the bureaucratic fabric of school life it's hard to imagine what schools were like before teachers' unions were formed, but it's important to know. Classroom teachers in the 1960s risked their jobs, paid heavy fines, and even went to jail to win the legal right to have organizations that would give them a voice in how schools are run. Their struggles gave teachers today many protections, such as limits on class size, that we take for granted. I think that in the years since they were organized, teachers' unions have weakened themselves by defining teachers' interests mainly in terms of economic issues, like salaries and pensions. City teacher unions have tended to lag behind advocacy groups in defending equality of educational opportunity. In fact, the unions have frequently become involved only *after* legislation has been passed, when the unions (correctly) point out the abuses and problems. Because the unions failed to be proactive in defending the rights of handicapped children and immigrant kids, they missed the opportunity to shape policy, to work with activists to try to put sensible and effective programs into schools.

The dynamic I describe above has characterized the relationship between urban teachers' unions and progressive social change for many years. Rather than being an ally and participant in the struggles of parent and community activists who are critical of schools for failing their kids, city teachers' unions, especially those in the largest cities, are often defensive. They remain neutral when struggles over equity issues arise, adopt a tepid position of support, or use their power to impede change. As a result, city teachers and their unions are often viewed by minority parents as opponents of school improvement. The unions are lumped together with politicians and corporate executives who control school systems, regarded as foes of real improvement. Part of the problem is not of the unions' making. They've just accommodated to the narrow role for teachers' unions spelled out in laws that establish collective bargaining.

It doesn't have to be that way, as I learned when I was active in my union local in California. The leaders of my local believed in and acted on the slogan "Teachers want what children need." I realize that it may be difficult for new teachers to imagine that the tired organizations they see in urban school systems today can be revitalized, and perhaps they can't with the existing leadership. But if teachers' unions don't find ways to work more creatively with allies in the communities that are not well served by urban schools, teachers will see their ability to influence what occurs in schools diminish.

As I was drafting this chapter, I had a casual conversation with a middle-class, European American father of two children about school in the city. The kids attended a well-regarded Manhattan public school regularly touted in the press for its high test scores and innovative curriculum. What is rarely mentioned in the media is that school serves an extraordinarily wealthy neighborhood. The father boasted about the quality of his kids' education and mentioned that the principal required all teachers in school to stay until 6:00 P.M. every day. When I suggested that this couldn't be the case, he corrected himself: The principal only hires those teachers who are willing to stay until 6:00 P.M. Earlier in our conversation he had mentioned that his wife taught special education in a Brooklyn school, one I knew was attended by working-class and poor children. As he extolled his children's school, I silently wondered if his wife stayed until 6:00 P.M. in *her* job, or whether she went home earlier to spend time with her family. I would never say that his wife *should* remain long past the end of the school day, because I believe that city teachers should not be forced to sacrifice a full personal life for their teaching. However, I was struck by the paradox and I hoped that his wife saw the contradiction between what they want and expect for their own children and the decisions teachers are forced to make about how much to do for the kids they teach.

As parents and citizens, we should be able to trust that schools value and respect the potential of all children. Under present conditions that happens only when city teachers make considerable sacrifices. Because of their knowledge of school life and their position within the school system, teachers are irreplaceable in the struggles that must occur to make urban schools the places they *should* be. As an urban teacher, shouldn't you be part of this effort to improve the place where you work and your students learn?

About the Author

After receiving her doctorate from the Harvard Graduate School of Education in 1990, Lois Weiner began teaching education at New Jersey City University, where she now coordinates a graduate program for experienced urban teachers. Her first book, *Preparing Teachers for Urban Schools* (Teachers College Press, 1993), was honored by the American Educational Research Association for its contribution to research on teacher education. Professor Weiner completed her undergraduate studies at the University of California, Berkeley and the University of Stockholm, Sweden, and her teaching preparation at California State University, Hayward. She received her M.A. from Teachers College, Columbia University. During the 15 years in which she taught high school English in California, in New York City, and in two suburbs of New York, she was an active member of the teachers' union. She lives in Manhattan with her daughter and husband and enjoys cooking and swimming year-round.